Dedicated to my adored Daddy, who is my earthly rock

and never-failing source of love and encouragement;

to my lovely, caring Mole, who turned my playroom into a schoolroom

and fostered in me a love of teaching from the age of four;

to Chloë and Tamsin, my beloved and beautiful girls,

who are the lights of my life and the apples of my eye

and to the many dyslexic youngsters who

put up with me practising spelling magic

on them and with them.

Getting started with 'Spelling Made Magic'

'Spelling Made Magic' is jam-packed with activities for you and your child to enjoy together. It has been designed to make spelling FUN, by making the most of the multi-sensory opportunities all around us. Multi-sensory learning is when you use as many senses as possible to create strong associations in your child's mind. I have been using multi-sensory learning methods to help children spell for over 20 years and I know that it works!

Traditionally, learning involved seeing and hearing; nowadays there is a lot more 'doing', using the kinesthetic or motor sense. 'Spelling Made Magic' involves using as many senses as possible – even the senses of taste and smell! This is why some of the exercises in 'Spelling Magic' include food! The more senses your children use in their learning, the more fun they will have and the more fun they have, the more memorable the learning.

Encourage your child to use any novelty pens they have, such as ones topped with feathers, glitter pens, scented pens or ones sporting their favourite cartoon characters. Anything that will lift writing from the ordinary to the extraordinary is like sprinkling their writing with magic dust! Add a pad of lined paper or a bright and cheerful exercise book, some A4 sheets of coloured paper and card, scissors, glue sticks and a well stocked pencil case. A little vocabulary book would be useful, too, as you will see in Chapter A.

Spelling Made Magic

An A-Z of spelling tips and tricks

Clare Winstanley

SPELLING MADE MAGIC – An A-Z of spelling tips and tricks

© Jade Creative 2012

All rights reserved. No part of this publication may be reproduced, stored in retrieval system, copied or transmitted without written permission from the publisher except that the materials may be photocopied for use within the purchasing institution only.

A catalogue record for this book is available from the British Library.

Written by:
Clare Winstanley

Edited by:
Amy Schofield

Design by:
Lorraine Gourlay

Printed by:
Hobbs the Printers Ltd
Brunel Road
Totton
Hampshire
SO40 3WX

Published by:
TheSchoolRun.com

Registered office:
60 St Margaret's Avenue, London, N20 9LJ

Registered number:
7940541

TheSchoolRun.com

ISBN 978-0-9565343-2-3

It is useful to have these items to hand as your essential Spelling Made Magic kit whenever you use this book:

- Pad of paper, lined, or exercise book
- Paper, plain and coloured
- Card, plain and coloured, or you can use old cereal boxes or Easter egg boxes
- Novelty pens (invest in smelly pens, gel pens, glitter pens, decorated furry or feather pens)
- Coloured pencils
- Crayons
- Poster paint
- PVA glue
- Scissors
- Alphabet letter stencils
- Old magazines/comics/mail order catalogues
- Old newspaper to protect your working surfaces
- Alphabetised book (such as an address book) to make an acrostics book
- Alphabetised book to make a vocabulary book

Each chapter also has a short list of extra optional items that you need to do all the activities in that chapter. Save pieces of bubble wrap, brightly coloured boxes from Easter eggs or biscuits, foil sweet wrappers and coloured tissue paper. Even unwanted photographs and negatives can be used, too! Dig out that old Etch-a-Sketch and that toy drum or xylophone. All these will be used to make spelling magic in the chapters ahead.

So, having collected together your kit, how should you begin?

- Designate a clean, uncluttered space for you and your child to work together, such as on the kitchen or dining table.

SPELLING MADE MAGIC – An A-Z of spelling tips and tricks

- Have your basic kit to hand – in an attractive storage box, if possible.
- Establish a relaxed and enjoyable environment with a drink and snack available.
- This is your special time together; try to limit interruptions.
- Aim for a 20 minute activity, as the brain learns most at the beginning and end of short activities. If your child is keen to continue, have a little break or play one of the games to vary the content.
- Depending on your time schedule, you could make spelling magic together for a short time every night, every other night or make it a weekend treat.
- Exude excitement and anticipation as you open the book so that your child looks forward to each new activity and associates learning with having fun.

Where should you start?

There is something for everyone in 'Spelling Made Magic'. The activities in it have been used by learners of all ages who have difficulties with spelling. However, your 5-year-old will not need to learn spelling rules just yet or how to chop long words into chunks. On the other hand, your 8- year-old may get a real buzz from being able to spell a long word like 'mediterranean' that might baffle his or her classmates!

I suggest that you as the parent read through Chapters A to C and see the sort of activities that are suggested. You may want to star the activities you think your child would enjoy and as you work through the chapters with them, keep reading the next chapter ahead to anticipate what would interest and benefit your child. The work your child brings home from school may guide you as to the most appropriate activities to tackle. Their reading book will give you an idea as to what words or sounds they need to work on and if they are given written homework to do, you will be able to spot any errors or areas of insecurity to tackle.

For example, if your young child confuses the letters 'b' and 'd' you can turn to Chapter B for a handy strategy (literally). Or if he does not understand why 'good' is pronounced 'gud' but not spelt that way, look at the relevant section in Chapter O. It is a good idea to ask your child's teacher what sounds they are working on in class so that you can reinforce them at home. Children are often given lists of spellings to learn at home. If the words have a common sound, such as the 'le' ending, look at the Contents page to see if the sound is covered or apply some of the activities you have read about in the book to help. Just writing the words out on an Etch-a-Sketch screen can make learning spellings fun rather than a chore.

Once your child is learning how to spell high frequency sight words – common words that do not sound as they spell, such as 'does' and 'said' – acrostics will be very useful. This is where a phrase is devised in which the first letter of each word spells out the tricky spelling. For example, 'does' can be remembered with the acrostic:

Does **O**liver **E**at **S**weets?

'Spelling Made Magic' contains a ready-made acrostic in each chapter but it is much more fun – and infinitely more memorable – to create your own. Each chapter also features a rule to help with spelling and a long word to chop up. It is often easier to spell long words than tricky shorter words like 'who' and 'does' because many long words are phonetically regular – that is, they are spelt as they sound.

Spelling long words, or 'polysyllabic spelling' as it is known, is a tremendous confidence booster. Your children will be so pleased with themselves when they can spell 17-letter long words with ease (see Chapter C). It will then seem a doddle to tackle those tricky little words using some of the tips and tricks in 'Spelling Made Magic'.

Although it is perfectly possible to work through 'Spelling Made Magic' systematically, certain chapters contain seasonal activities. Therefore, before Christmas, Easter and Bonfire Night have a look at the activities in the relevant chapters. Ideas for celebrating festivals from other faiths are included in Chapter F. You can treat 'Spelling Made Magic' as a 'Pick and Mix' resource and dip in and out of different chapters. If a strategy or activity refers to a previous chapter you can simply go back to it.

Every chapter contains a variety of games, activities and spelling strategies. You can judge whether your child can cope with all the different items or whether to revisit some of them at a later date. Certainly, if your child is aged seven and above, most of the activities should be appropriate and you can simply work through the chapters. On the other hand, once you have worked through chapters A – C, you could always dip in and out of the chapters and choose an activity that catches your eye, like a magician pulling a rabbit out of a hat! Or your child may like to choose a letter of the alphabet and look at the activities in that chapter. It's up to you! What is important is to have fun together as you and your child enjoy 'Spelling Made Magic'.

Why using all the senses boosts your child's spelling

Sight and hearing are generally the two senses most cited for use in learning, so it may seem odd to think that learning takes all the senses. However, the senses of touch, movement, smell and imagination can all help your child learn in ways you may never have thought possible.

Multi-sensory learning is already used to aid children with learning difficulties such as dyslexia, along with more severe learning disabilities. Around 10% of the population have dyslexia, a learning difference which affects the way reading, spelling and writing are learnt. Alternative learning methods, using the different senses, can help such learners learn effectively rather than struggling with common literacy learning styles. It is thought that around 20% of learners struggle with traditional reading, spelling and listening so there is much to suggest that multi-sensory teaching and learning practices help unlock a child's potential.

According to educational experts, using as many senses as possible encourages stronger associations and association is a proven accelerated learning tool. It's fun to utilise the senses of touch, taste and smell in learning. Pre-school children learn through play, so why should older children not be allowed to do so, too? When we're having fun, we relax and when we relax we learn so much more easily.

Children can use complementary methods such as movement, tactile learning and music to learn effectively. Depending on the sensory method used, this extra added dimension to lessons can help children with repetition, motor skills and memory which, in turn, aid spelling, handwriting, and literacy.

We all have different ways of learning: some of us are visual learners, some of us are auditory and some of us prefer kinaesthetic (physical) ways of learning, so using a multisensory teaching approach means helping a child to learn through using more than one of the senses. It's a great way to help children, particularly dyslexic children, to learn to read and spell.

How multi-sensory learning works

By using different senses, learning can be aided in new ways. If your child is struggling with literacy, employing a new sense can help to add a new perspective to a topic. The idea is that your child can use a multi-dimensional approach rather than traditional repetition methods (look, learn by rote, repeat).

Multi-sensory methods can be used individually or combined. Some children may respond better to some methods than others, so it's important to be prepared to try out different styles to see what works best with your child.

One multi-sensory activity that you will find in Chapter B of this book is to give a child who is spelling short, tricky words a piece of bubble wrap; they click the letters into their memories by popping a bubble as they sound out or name each letter aloud. They should always start and finish by saying the word that they have spelt so that they associate the letters with that word. It is important that the child hears himself saying the word and the letter names aloud because the 'self voice' has been proven to be the best teacher. If you ask him how to spell that word he should remember hearing himself say that very word and the letters that spelt it.

Other multi-sensory methods, and how they can be used, include:

Audio – this can work in two ways; singing can help children learn spellings (think chanting 'M - i -double s - i - double s – i – double p – i' to spell 'Mississippi') and enable them to 'sound out' in their head. Listening to music both aids relaxation and stimulates the brain which helps visual and auditory senses; recordings of poetry or stories that children are working on also helps children mentally process and understand the piece of work.

Visual – digital camcorders enable children to film themselves, play back and assess how they have done, a technique that can help children to increase their confidence by seeing how they have completed a task. The film can also be used to show how progress has continued.

Touch – Children can learn to process information by being able to feel what they are doing, such as practising writing in sand or on carpet with their fingers, or making letters using modelling clay.

Movement – also known as Educational Kinesiology, which is movement combined with learning, includes using natural core and motor skills to improve areas such as memory, concentration, handwriting and communication skills.

Smell – introducing the 'smells' of a topic; such as what would a particular environment smell like, would it be fresh, sour, delicious, unpleasant? The smell response can evoke ideas that can be used in storytelling and give meaning to words.

Kinaesthetic imagination – discussing how something would feel, sound or smell like to evoke an imaginative response, thus widening your child's vocabulary.

SPELLING MADE MAGIC – An A-Z of spelling tips and tricks

How do these methods of multi-sensory learning help a child learn?

Consider how you read or write a story. Think about the way a scene is set and the responses it evokes. Multi-sensory techniques add to a child's literacy by helping them use their imagination for creative storytelling including the use of their characters, character's language and scene setting by giving your child the tools with which to describe what the character might see, say or feel.

In other topics, these techniques can aid memory by putting an extra dimension to the topic. Instead of just reading about a period of history, they can visualise and imagine how costumes might feel or they might listen to how music of that period sounded or taste a popular food of the time. Similarly, chanting or singing difficult spellings can help the mind absorb spellings which then gives a greater chance of writing the words correctly. Imaginative learning helps to give a topic a '3D' feel. This gives greater impact to their class work when writing a story set in that period or giving descriptive answers to questions about the work.

One teacher taught her 8-year-olds where the Vikings came from in a rap marching and giggling round the classroom dressed up as Vikings singing to 'Sweden, Norway, Denmark…where they come from…?' This works because if you engage all the senses, learning becomes far more enjoyable and the unconscious kicks in and remembers much more.

Many of these techniques can be used easily at home and will certainly make homework more entertaining for keen but struggling children or unenthusiastic learners.

Using sand, or glittery salt in a tray (see Chapter S) to help children to learn to write their letters with their hands, or drawing letters and words on each other's backs can all help your child to use their senses to improve their spelling. Another useful and fun activity is to make letters out of modelling clay, cookie dough or fudge, all of these activities you will find in the pages of 'Spelling Made Magic'. For example, try the gingerbread dough activity in Chapter G to tackle the soft 'ge' and 'gi' sounds. Children will associate the gingerbread with the soft 'g' words they spell using the cooked letters. Your child really will be eating their words!

How do these methods aid spelling?

Traditionally, literacy has been taught by sight and hearing. Chunks of text are read and repeated with the idea that the ability to read and write is absorbed and developed. Once reading and writing is mastered, spelling becomes important, especially when homophones (their, they're, there) can change meanings.

However, not everyone learns well by rote. By introducing the touch sense on a tactile surface, or by forming the letters using dough, children can practice their spelling and also have a greater connection to the way letters are formed. In turn, this helps them absorb the way letters are formed and the correct way of spelling.

Perhaps best of all for children who are struggling to unlock their potential, is that they learn that multi-sensory learning is fun. It enables them to move, sing, touch, smell and play imaginatively, thus taking away the idea that learning is dull. With multi-sensory learning, it is anything but!

A is for autumn, acrostics and alphabet arcs!

Extra materials needed:

- Large wooden or plastic letters, or small magnetic letters
- Roll of sugar paper or old wallpaper
- Autumn leaves (if in season)

Alphabet Arcs

A brilliant introductory activity to any spelling session is to ask your child to put the letters of the alphabet into an arc or rainbow. Some big plastic or wooden letters are ideal for this, or some of the smaller, magnetic letters that are readily available. To help with the structure of the arc, ask your child what is in the middle of their face! If necessary, point it out to them so that they reply, "My nose." Thus, the middle letters of the alphabet – letters 'm' and 'n' - go in the middle of the arc at the highest point. The letters 'a' and 'z' obviously start and finish the arc. Performing this activity enables you to check that your child knows which way the letters face, which letters correspond to which name and in which order they go.

Acrostics

These are poems or sentences where the first letter of each word or line spells a word. For example, the spelling of 'through' can be remembered as:

Ten

Hairy

Round

Oranges

Use

Green

Hairspray.

I love making up weird and wonderful acrostics that stick in the mind and help with the spelling of those awkward medium and high frequency sight words. Encourage your child to devise his or her own acrostics, as that way they take ownership of the spelling and are much more likely to remember it. One of my favourites was devised by a boy who was struggling to remember the spelling of 'isosceles'. He came up with:

I Sit **O**n **S**oft **C**ushions **E**ating **L**ovely **E**gg **S**andwiches

It conjures up a luxurious, luscious picture every time I think of it!

Give your child a book to write the acrostics in. An alphabetised book, such as an address book, would facilitate speedy retrieval. If your child enjoys drawing, they could draw a picture of their acrostic so that they can more easily picture or visualise the spelling and the picture conveyed by the acrostic. This becomes a multi-sensory activity that aids accelerated learning. To maximise the learning process, encourage your child to look through the book regularly to refresh their memory for the spellings.

Al and Ally

A hugely successful and fun activity is to draw around a boy and a girl on separate rolls of sugar paper and cut out the figures. These become 'Al' and 'Ally'. Make adjectives (words that describe nouns) by adding 'al' to words, as though you are describing a boy called 'Al'. So, 'electric Al' becomes 'electrical'; 'magic Al' becomes 'magical'; 'music Al' becomes 'musical' and so on. Make jig-cards of the syllables (mu-sic-al) and muddle them up for your child to put together and stick on Al, so that they get used to chopping words into chunks or syllables (syllabification). This will help them read and spell long words.

Then add 'Ally' to the same words to make adverbs (words that describe verbs or doing words). This is particularly helpful, because so often the words are pronounced as though there is no 'a' in the suffix. 'Practically' is usually pronounced 'practicly' and 'comically' is pronounced 'comicly'. Teaching the syllabification of these words is not enough; the youngsters need to know that 'al' becomes 'ally' when converting adjectives to adverbs. Again, make the syllables of the adverbs into jig-cards to place on Ally.

Autumn

The autumn term is the ideal month to deal with the vowel phoneme 'au'. You could draw or press autumn leaves and stick them on a tree outline as a display. Ask your child to find 'au' words and write, type or stencil them onto slips of paper to stick on a leaf. Then play a guessing game asking the youngster which word you have written down. They could practise their spelling by writing down on a whiteboard the word they think you have chosen and then choose a word for you to guess in the same way.

Nearer Christmas revise the 'au' digraph with a Santa Claus display, perhaps with words written on a parcel or baubles on a Christmas tree that your children have cut out and decorated.

Advanced spelling

To help older children remember the silent 'n' at the end of 'autumn', remind them of the 'al' adjective 'autumnal', as in 'an autumnal morning', where it is easy to hear the 'n'. Later, when your child is studying science at secondary school, it is easy to remember the chemical symbol for gold (Au) with reference to autumn when the leaves turn gold!

Angels v Angles

This is not quite a homophone (where two words sound the same but have different spellings, like 'two' and 'too') but children easily and understandably confuse them. I used to suggest that children think of the word 'angelic' to hear the 'g-e-l' sound in 'angel', but one of my pupils told me quite categorically that angels have gel in their hair. I now visualise the heavenly host with an array of wonderful and creative hairstyles so the spelling has now 'stuck' in the mind! (Please pardon the pun…)

A tricky word: Argument

This word is often spelt 'arguement', because of its root 'argue', or 'agrument'. Chopping it into the syllables - ar/gu/ment - and remembering to spell each syllable as simply as possible ('gu' rather than 'gue') should help. It's also fun to point out the word 'gum' within it and suggest that two people had an argument over some gum!

SPELLING MADE MAGIC – An A-Z of spelling tips and tricks

An 'A' rule

'All' has only one 'l' when followed by another syllable.

also	almost	altogether
already	always	although

(You could also teach them 'almighty', which children often associate with the film 'Bruce Almighty' and the old-fashioned word for 'although' - 'albeit'.)

Spelling game

Your child may enjoy making a Pairs game with the words above. They could type each word four times using a different font, so that they get used to looking carefully at the letters that make up these words. Alternatively, they could use different stencils or just different coloured felt tip pens.

Having stuck these words on small rectangles of card (7cm x 5cm is a good size), you can now spread out the cards, shuffled up, face down on the table and take it in turns to pick up two cards, aiming to find a pair of words. If you pick a pair you can have another go! Often children's memories are much quicker than ours and you may find that your child will wipe the board of pairs, leaving you with none. This will do wonders for their confidence but may seriously knock yours! Perhaps maximum of three goes per player before the next player has a chance to play would be more fair! As well as consolidating the 'al' rule and familiarising your child with these spellings, it will develop memory strategies in you and your child alike.

Auditory learning:

Use the 'Spelling Sandwiches' method to learn spellings! This method adds the oral/aural senses to the popular, multi-sensory Look, Cover, Write and Check method. When the child is going to 'Write' the word, encourage him to say it aloud, (the first slice of bread), then name the letters aloud that make up the word as he writes them, (the filling), and then sandwich the whole thing together by saying the word aloud again and checking that he is correct. The process is repeated four times.

This method is effective because the child hears his own voice spelling out the word and by repeating the whole word at the end, he anchors the letters to the word, so that he knows that g-o-n-e spells 'gone' and not 'goes'. It is almost like self-hypnosis in that when the child thinks "How do I spell 'gone'?" he should remember hearing himself saying the letters "g-o-n-e" after the word.

The 'self-voice' has been proven to be the most effective teacher and I can think of innumerable students who have cracked previously 'unmemorable' words in this way. It encourages automaticity and confidence. If the child is hesitant or has to search for the letters when I am testing them, I can tell they have not been using this technique, even if they insist they have!

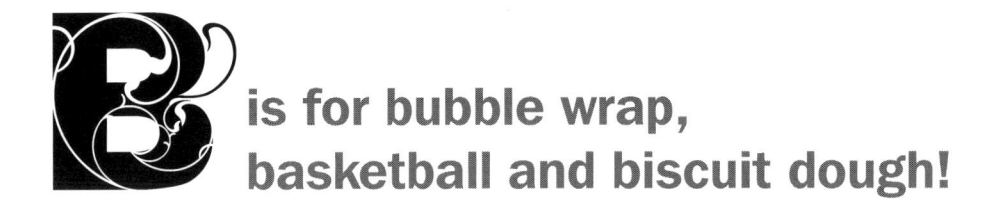

B is for bubble wrap, basketball and biscuit dough!

Extra materials needed:

- Bubble wrap

- Ball of any size

- Mini-basketball net

- Biscuit dough (buy ready-made or make your own)

- Glitter (or iridescent nail varnishes)

- Dice

Pop your child's brain into action

When learning short, tricky sight words, a novel, kinaesthetic way to 'click' the letters into the memory is to pop a bubble in a piece of bubble wrap as you sound out or name each letter. There are hundreds of nerve endings in the fingertips and stimulating them through pressure stimulates the brain. That's the scientific rationale, but apart from the science bit, it's such fun and so multi-sensory. The novelty value alone makes it a memorable activity, but it is probably best avoided with a group of children together or it could sound as if a room full of pop guns is going off!

Have a bounce around in the fresh air

Just for a change, take your child outside for a spelling session. They'll remember this activity – and probably ask to repeat it time after time. They can practise spelling their tricky words or their spellings for the week by bouncing a netball or basketball, or any ball for that matter, saying a letter with each bounce and then saying the word while they aim the basketball into the net. I have a mini basketball net I take around with me for my pupils and they love aiming a tennis ball into it while I move it around to ensure they get it through the net! Another benefit is that it does wonders for their hand/eye co-ordination. It is a great way for children to actively learn.

Eat up your words!

Alternatively, take your children into the kitchen and get them literally eating their words. The children can't get enough of them! You could combine this with a cookery lesson and the kids can make their own biscuit dough. Then the children can fashion the dough into the letters to spell their words of the week. A word to the wise: be prepared for plenty of giggling if you choose chocolate or gingerbread dough, as in their uncooked state these letters can look most, how can I put this, unsavoury!

Seasonal spellings

As well as the potential Bonfire Night offers for beautiful artistic work, it can also stimulate wonderfully creative approaches to spelling. You can brainstorm a multitude of describing words to capture the sounds and sights of the bonfire or the fireworks, extending your child's vocabulary by suggesting more sophisticated colours such as azure, magenta, crimson, scarlet and chestnut.

Write words in the sky

Try firework spelling or spelling sparklers. Brainstorm spellings with the same pattern and write them in the style of spelling sparklers, with the words shooting out of the first word and decorate them with coloured sparks.

Reality TV check

Figures from popular books, the television and the cinema can provide inspiration.

Big Brother had its uses! I wanted to teach the 'le' sound one summer and was delighted that one of the contestants on Big Brother at that time was called 'Bubble'. We made a display, entitled 'the Big Brother Bubble Bath', featuring a cut-out bath, with Bubble's head reclining at one end and lots of bubbles, cut out of OHP transparencies and decorated lightly with iridescent nail varnishes and a 'le' word, heaped up in the bath. We stuck pictures of the different contestants on individual bubbles and as they were evicted from the show the appropriate bubble floated out of the bath.

B/d confusion thumbs up

It isn't just dyslexic youngsters who confuse the letters b and d. An easy way to demonstrate the difference between them is to ask your child to give you the thumbs up with both hands. The left hand thus forms the 'b' shape and the right hand forms the 'd' shape. A good trick to help your child to remember which is which is to put the hands together and, voila, you have made the shape of a bed, which begins with the 'b' sound and ends with the 'd' sound!

Another method is to hear the 'b' sound at the beginning of 'bat' and 'ball'. When you form the letter you start with the long, slim bat, then attach the ball on the side. Similarly, for the 'd', think of a drum with a stick. This time, when you form the letter you begin with the round drum then add the stick at the side. Sorted!

A trick for a tricky word: believe

To ensure the inclusion of the 'i' in 'believe' teach your child, "Never believe a lie."

B acrostics

Big elephants proliferate in my acrostics! Most youngsters know at least one acrostic for 'because'. 'Big Elephants Can Add Up Sums Easily' is preferable to 'Big Elephants Can't Always Use Small Exits' or 'Big Elephants Can Always Upset

Small Elephants' for younger children who have not yet learnt to spell 'always', beginning with 'al' rather than 'or'. An alternative is 'Billy Eats Cakes At Uncle Sam's Engine'.

My favourite acrostic for older youngsters who can spell 'always' is for the word 'beautiful': 'Big Elephants Always Use Turquoise Ink For Underlining Letters'. Once again it conjures up a memorable (and surreal) picture that your child might also like to draw or paint.

'B' homophones: by, buy and bye

Help your child to distinguish between 'by' and 'buy' by remembering the 'u' in 'buy', with the question, "Where did you buy that?"

Explain that 'Goodbye' comes from 'God be with ye', so put the 'b' with 'ye'.

And finally...

Don't forget that invaluable and addictive spelling aid – bingo! All my private lessons with primary school children end with the obligatory game of bingo – at their insistence. Whether it is a number lesson or a literacy lesson out come the 'blobbers', as one of my pupils calls them. We play tables bingo with a 12 sided die or addition bingo with two dice, and play spelling bingo with a selection of key words on cards to choose and match with the words we have written on our pre-printed grids. I often played bingo with my primary school classes, using key words from our topics, whether History, Geography, Science or RE. It gave the children practice writing and reading these key words and was totally addictive – try it at home!

Conjures up Christmas and chocolate!

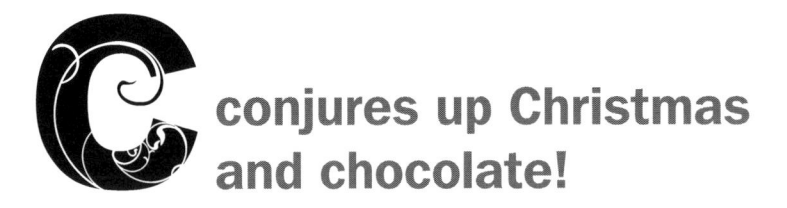

Extra materials:

- Paperclips
- Christmas baubles
- Scraps of Christmas paper
- Candles

My whole philosophy of spelling and reading long words was originally encapsulated in a Christmas cake. Unfortunately, many of the youngsters with whom I have worked have wrinkled up their noses when I have started talking about rich, fruity Christmas cakes – so now I have resorted to using a large, party-sized chocolate gateau, which is much more popular and seems to go down very well!

The principle is this: like the poor boy in Roald Dahl's 'Matilda', most of us would struggle to eat a huge, creamy, chocolate gateau in one go without feeling very ill.

Similarly, for some children, trying to read or spell long words makes them feel uncomfortable, sweaty or sick – or all three. It makes far more sense to chop up a cake into chunks and tackle it a chunk at a time, in your own time. So it is with words.

Chop long words up into chunks or syllables and often the syllables will sound out quite easily and an impressively long word can be built up with no stress. It is also a most effective way of building confidence, promoting competence and boosting a child's self-esteem.

Suggest to your child you start with a lovely long 17-letter word! Without telling them the word, enable them to build up the word 'misunderstandings'. Using the biggest plastic or wooden letters you have, start letter by letter and then speed things up. First, spell 'a', then add a letter to make it 'an', then 'and', 'sand' and 'stand' and then make the word say 'standing'. Spell the word 'under' and slide it in front of 'standing' to give 'understanding'. Using this technique, you are gradually building up the long word by adding manageable "slices".

At intervals ask your child to count how many letters you have used and how many more letters you need to reach 17 (sneaking in a crafty bit of numeracy when they're not looking!) Next, ask them - what is the opposite of 'understanding'? Answer - 'misunderstanding'. They should spell the prefix as simply as they can, using three letters, add a final 's' to turn it into the plural and without even realising it they have easily spelt a 17-letter long word (just watch out that the letters don't all end up on the floor!)

Clearly, one would not spell such a word letter by letter. It makes so much more sense to chop the word into chunks for your child, to divide it into mis/un/der/stand/ings.

Encourage your child to photograph each syllable with their mental camera and when they feel ready, muddle up the letters and put them back into order. Those who are competitive enjoy being timed putting the word back together and trying to beat their time in successive lessons.

A wealth of wonderful words

Once your child has got the hang of chopping words such as 'computer', 'calculating' and 'development' up into regular syllables and spelling them as simply as they can, introduce them to the 'tion' suffix and they will enter an Aladdin's cave of wonderful words. If they are tempted to spell 'tion' as 'shun' help them by reminding them that in schools where ties are part of the uniform they will be told off if they have not got their 'ti(e) on'.

Contractions

From big words to small ones – contractions are words made when two words have been squashed or contracted together. You can tell when this has been done because of the tell-tale apostrophe in the word. For example,

don't   couldn't   won't   I'll   you've

Most youngsters quickly cotton on to the need for apostrophes but sometimes put them in the wrong place. In the case of 'don't' they realise that the two words squashed together are 'do not' and, very intelligently, think there is a space between 'do' and 'not', so put the apostrophe there : do'nt.

A little activity that helps simply requires some slips of paper and paperclips to help to iron out the confusion.

Write out the two words on a slip of paper.

do not

When we contract the two words 'do not' to one word 'don't', we miss out the 'o' sound in 'not'. Fold the paper so that the 't' covers the 'o' and hold it in place with a paperclip. This shows your child where the apostrophe would go.

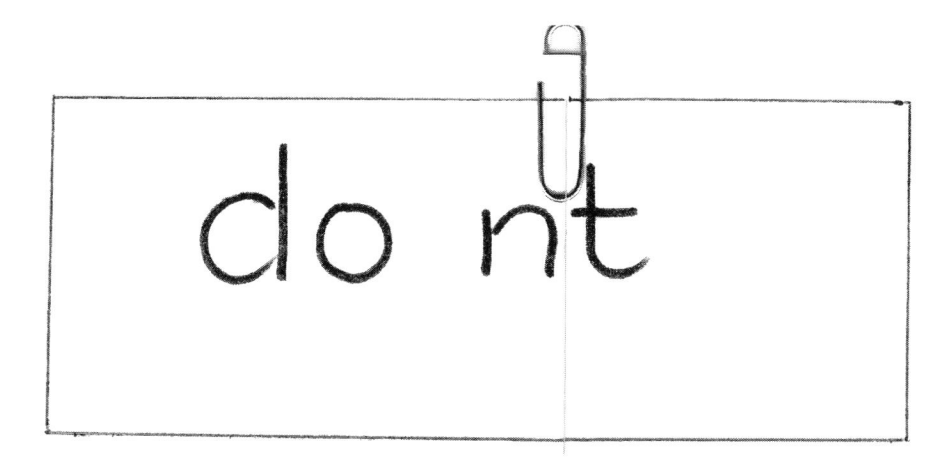

Then, when writing the word 'don't', we leave out the space between 'do' and 'n't. Simple!

Your child can have fun thinking of all the contractions we use in everyday speech. In fact, it could be a novel form of homework for them to listen to people talking and jot down all the contractions they can hear and see how many they can record in an hour – or even longer if they enjoy the activity.

Then they can analyse the contractions and see which words have been contracted to make them. Usually, contractions are formed from 'not' combinations and from the verbs 'to be' and 'to have'.

have not	–	haven't	are not	–	aren't
did not	–	didn't	could not	–	couldn't
should not	–	shouldn't	would not	–	wouldn't
And the interesting variant			will not	–	won't
I have	–	I've	you have	–	you've

she has	–	she's		he has	–	he's etc
I am	–	I'm		I will	–	I'll
you are	–	you're		you will	–	you'll etc

Your child may then like to do the "paperclip trick". (Anything that sounds as if it involves magic usually makes it more 'fun' rather than simply 'educational' and children are much more likely to want to do it!)

Another activity to reinforce understanding would be to make a Pairs game where you have to match up a card featuring the two uncontracted words with a card bearing the contraction. There! That's sorted!

Coding vowels

It is very important that your child understands whether the vowels in a word are long or short. If we begin with 'cvc' (consonant, vowel, consonant) words like 'cat' and 'dog', the short sound 'a' and 'o' can be heard. These words are only one syllable long and they are known as 'closed syllables'. Tell your child that the vowel has been closed in by the last consonant.

If there is no consonant after the vowel, as in the words: 'me', 'go' and 'hi', the syllable is called an open syllable and the vowel sound can go on as long as it likes, so it is a long vowel. Ask your child to listen to the difference in the vowel sounds between such words as 'leg' and 'he', 'big' and 'I'. 'hot' and 'no'. Note that 'y' is a half vowel so words like 'sky' are open syllables.

When there are two or even three consonants at the end of a word, so the pattern is 'cvcc', the vowel is still enclosed by consonants so the syllable is closed and the vowel sound is short. For example, 'black', 'soft', 'next' and so on.

The way to code these vowel sounds, to help us use them in future activities, is to use a macron and a breve. A macron looks like a smile drawn above the vowel and signifies that the vowel is short. A breve is just a line drawn above the vowel and indicates the vowel is long. So the coding rule is 'Smile for short and line for long.' Ask your child to code the vowels in these words: hat, peg, so, she, dog, sit, try, go, luck, be, pinch, dry, do, song, bench, fox, sky, we, rod and fun. Now fold a piece of paper into 2 columns. Write 'short vowel' at the top of one column and 'long vowel' at the top of the other. Ask your child to write these words in the correct columns, using their codes to help them.

A 'c' acrostic: 'colour'

This word trips so many children up. I was so thankful to a national DIY store a year or so ago which had an advertising campaign featuring

'our

colours'.

I was so tempted to 'borrow' one of their huge advertising boards to use as a spelling aid! However, I restrained myself and continued to use the following acrostic

Carry **O**ld **L**adies **O**ver **U**neven **R**oads.

Or, if your child prefers and can picture this more readily, substitute lions for ladies!

A homophone for older children: council/counsel

Think of the phrase 'wise counsel' and remember they both have an 'e'.

If it doesn't teach cynicism you could say that the council always has to dot the 'i's and cross the 't's!

A 'c' word to syllabify: con/den/sa/tion

A 'c' rule: Change the 'y' to an 'i' when you add an ending (unless the suffix begins with 'i')

This rule helps us understand why 'business' is spelt the way it is. The word is troublesome because it clearly sounds as though the 'i' is in the first syllable. Often youngsters spell the word 'buisness', their visual memory reminding them of the 'u' and perhaps thinking of the word 'build'. If we take the word back to its root – 'busyness' and apply the rule 'change the y to an 'i' we can see how it becomes 'business'. Once one understands the rule, other words become clear e.g. beautiful, marriage and carriage.

Cursive script

Did you know that your hand has a memory?

When you are driving you don't have to consciously think about moving the gear stick up or down the gears; your hand knows what to do. Cursive script (joined up writing) engages the memory of the hand for spelling. The 'feel' of the joined up letters in the word 'where', for example, will differ markedly from that of the word 'wear'. So once your child has mastered the basics of cursive writing, encourage him to use it when practising his spellings so that he commits the word to the memory of the hand.

Consolidation

Remember! It is vital to revisit, review and consolidate any new work for optimum learning.

It is often helpful to look at something from a different angle. In the A chapter, we covered the 'au' vowel digraph, which is not a very common blend, with reference to autumn. Now would be a great time to consolidate it with reference to Santa Claus! You could have a picture of Santa Claus' head sticking out of a chimney, with different 'au' words on the bricks of the chimney, or a Christmas tree with beautifully decorated baubles, each featuring an 'au' word.

Alternatively, teach the 'le' ending with a selection of 'le' words on the baubles or on a collection of candles. An old-fashioned candle-holder containing a candle can be drawn in such a way that it resembles an 'le'.

candle

look at the handle
on the candle

Christmas words

Usually, the 'l' ending is spelt 'le'. Three of the words associated with Christmas end in 'el' – 'parcel', 'tinsel' and 'angel' so it is worth learning them together.

A favourite Christmas display that can come out year after year with new or more sophisticated words added is the picture of a huge cracker, pulled into two jagged halves. Out of the cracker is exploding a host of smaller crackers in different colours, each featuring an 'er' word, such as 'manger', 'paper', 'computer' and so on. Cut the crackers out of different coloured paper or Christmas wrapping paper scraps.

D stands for drums, dice and dominoes!

Extra materials needed:

- Drum
- Blank playing cards, or make your own from coloured card
- Connect 4 or similar counters game
- Old magazines or comics
- Dice

It also stands for a group of people who are very dear to me – dyslexics. Having worked with dyslexic children and adults for more than 15 years, it has become second nature to make my lessons as multi-sensory as possible, because dyslexics learn best through a combination of the senses – seeing, hearing, saying, doing and even on occasion smelling and eating! This is known as 'accelerated learning'.

Accelerated learning involves using as many senses as possible and works because of the power of association and the use of both halves of the brain.

Traditionally, we use the left hemisphere of the brain when learning in school, focusing on words, numbers, logic and sequences whereas the right hemisphere of the brain deals with colour, pictures, music, rhyme and rhythm.

You would think that if we just used one half of our brain we would be using our brain to 50% of its capacity, but in fact it has been proved that we only use it to between 5 and 10% of its capacity! To maximise learning, we need to use both halves of the brain together. Multi-sensory lessons stimulate both halves of the brain. So, what is good for dyslexics is good for all!

For example, we can use rhythm to help with learning tables, spellings or rules. (Look in the W chapter for a use of rhythm to help spell one of the worst words in the English language – in my opinion!) Many parents will remember chanting their tables as I did; we were carried along by the rhythm and the tables were anchored by it.

Drumming out spellings

Try putting tricky spellings to a rhythm and getting your child to play the rhythm on a drum. Perhaps do this when the neighbours are out, though!

If you don't happen to have a set of drums, why not make your own? Improvise by using empty cans or jars or resorting to the much loved childhood favourite of banging a wooden spoon on upturned saucepans, while sounding out the spellings of the day. The point of this exercise is to make spelling fun, a hands-on activity that will be memorable by association. Association is an accelerated learning tool and your child will associate those spellings with the drumming and be more likely to remember them.

Of course, other instruments can be used – a tambourine could be a quieter option, or a pair of castanets or even some chopsticks! Be creative and find different ways to put spellings to a rhythm.

In 'Matilda', Roald Dahl quotes a popular way of remembering to spell 'difficulty', by using the following chant:

Mrs D

Mrs I

Mrs FFI

Mrs C

Mrs U

Mrs LTY.

A 'd' rule: Drop the 'e' when you add 'ing'

This has a catchy rhythm that can be clapped as a reminder to apply the rule with the following words, for example:

Drop the 'e' when you add 'ing'.

Bake – baking	interfere – interfering
Like – liking	smoke – smoking
Ride – riding	rule – ruling

Give your child the task of finding 20 verbs (doing words) that end in 'e'. The above could start them off and trigger other examples. Then ask them to write down 30 verbs that do not end in 'e'. Write these on a pack of blank playing cards, available from some stationers, or make your own from coloured card. This spelling activity also uses the game of Connect 4 or a similar counters dropping game:

SPELLING MADE MAGIC – An A-Z of spelling tips and tricks

You will need

Your 50 verb cards

Connect 4 game or similar counters game

Paper

Pencils

Shuffle the 50 verb cards and place them face down on the table. Both players must fold their paper into two columns headed 'Drop the e' and 'No e'. Take it in turns to take a card, then write down the verb+ing in the correct column. For every word they correctly write in the 'Drop the e' column they can drop a counter into the Connect 4 grid and try to make a row of 4.

This can also be played with more than two players but without Connect 4. The winner is the first to get a pre-determined number of words in the 'Drop the e' column. If you run out of cards, shuffle the pack and use the cards again.

Days of the week activity

It is a good idea to make a calendar so that every day your child can change the day and the date. They could stencil out the names of the days and the months and have a chart saying 'Today is the   (day), the   (date), of the   (month).

The order of the days of the week could be learnt by reading and reciting the rhyme (slightly altered from the traditional version):

Monday's child is fair of face,

Tuesday's child is full of grace.

Wednesday's child is full of woe

Thursday's child has far to go.

Friday's child is loving and giving.

Saturday's child works hard for a living.

But the child that is born on a **Sunday**

Is bonny and blithe, come what may.

If your child is good at drawing or enjoys colouring pictures, they could draw a different child for each day, or look through magazines and comics to find people with appropriate expressions and stick those on the chart.

Your youngster may like to research the origins of the names of the days of the week on the internet or you may like to read them stories of the gods who gave their name to the days, as a little historical background. Wednesday is derived from 'Woden's day', the chief Anglo-Saxon god, while Thursday should really be 'Thor's day', the Norse god of thunder. Freya, who gave her name to Friday, was the Teutonic goddess of love and beauty.

Name displays for vocabulary extension

It is worth capitalising on names and making displays around your child's name or surname. Your child can write and decorate their name as attractively as possible and put it at the hub of a display with words that rhyme with it shooting out from it. So, Paul could inspire a host of 'au' words, Sue a collection of 'ue' words, Clare – 'are' words, Josh – 'sh' words and so on.

Surnames often provide similar opportunities for creative vocabulary extension. Brown helps with the 'ow' sound, Jones with the silent 'e' (more of that in the next chapter) and Smith with the 'th' sound, especially if your child tends to pronounce 'th' as 'f'. I once had a pupil with the wonderful surname, Cloudsdale, and we made a display of lots of fluffy white clouds on a blue background, with a different 'ou' word on each cloud.

Spelling dice game

A spelling exercise that incorporates a little maths involves making two cubes of card (use the template on page 30), and making them into spelling dice.

On the faces of one die, for an example, you could put the initial consonant blends bl, cl, fl, br, tr, sh and on the other die you could put a variety of endings, such as 'ack', 'ick', 'ock', 'ank', 'ink' and 'ash'.

Players take it in turns to shake the dice and see how many 'real' words they can produce. The first player to write down a certain number of real words is the winner.

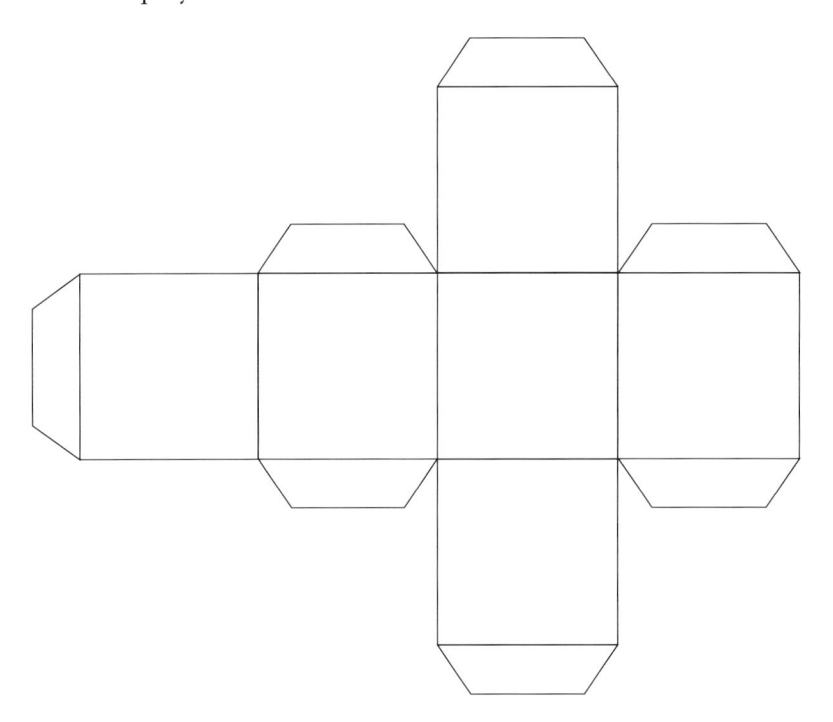

A 'd' acrostic: does

Does **O**liver **E**at **S**weets?

'Does' is a tricky word and so many children want to spell this 'dose'. Similarly, 'goes' is often and intelligently spelt 'gose', as though rhyming with 'nose' and 'rose'.

You may approach these words in two ways:

First, teach the string of two letter words ending in 'o':

so, no, go, to, do

(If it's Christmas time, you could add Santa Claus' catchphrase "Ho, ho, ho!") When your child is familiar with those, you can go on to tackle the 'do' and 'go' families, in parallel fashion.

go	do
going	doing
gone	done
goes	does

A 'd' homophone: diary / dairy.

Strictly speaking, these words are not really homophones because they do not sound alike, but because they contain the same letters they are sometimes confused.

The simplest way to emphasise the difference between them is to divide them into their component syllables.

Di/a/ry clearly has 3 but 'dair/y only has 2.

It could be helpful to do some work on words that rhyme with 'air' and then add 'dairy' and 'fairy'.

A 'd' word to syllabify: de/scrip/tion

One of the rules of syllabification is (generally) to spell each syllable as simply as possible. Bearing this in mind, it is tempting to spell 'description' or 'decide', as 'd/scrip/tion' and 'd/cide.'

A crucial rule in syllabification is that every syllable must have a vowel – 'a', 'e',' i', 'o' or 'u'. Therefore, 'description' and 'decide' are spelt 'de'.

The problem is that both words sound as though they begin with 'dis'. Teach your child that 'dis' means the opposite. So 'disagree' is the opposite of 'agree' and 'dislike' is the opposite of 'like'. If it is not an opposite it should be spelt 'de…'.

Extension exercise

There are always exceptions to the rule, such as 'disturb' and 'disaster', but you and your child could do a little exploratory work in the 'd' section of a dictionary and discuss the exceptions as an extension exercise.

Another way to help your child remember to spell 'describe' with an 'e' rather than an ' i ' is to think of the phrase:

Des described his ideal car.

Dominoes game

Together with your child, make 20 dominoes out of card, with 'de' on the right hand side of 10 dominoes and 'dis' on the right hand side of the other 10. Write the following endings on the left hand sides:

'cember', 'stroy', 'scend', 'serve', 'sign', 'sire', 'spair', 'spise', 'spite', 'scribe', believe', 'obey', 'organised', 'able', 'agree', 'appear', appoint', 'honest', 'loyal' and 'cover'.

Just writing these out will help your child to identify the 'real' words that can be paired with their opposites.

Meanwhile, you now have a collection of dominoes that you can divide between the players and take it in turns to add a domino to make a legitimate word.

agree	dis

obey	de

sign	de

E stands for Easter eggs and an enormous mouse!

Extra materials needed:

- Old Easter egg boxes or any colourful boxes made of card
- Foil (foil from Easter eggs or chocolate wrappers is ideal)
- String of beads
- Roll of sugar paper or old wallpaper
- Stick or magic wand from dressing-up
- Ribbons, streamers, glitter

I love Easter time for many reasons but for children it tends to mean that the shops are full of gaudy and bright Easter eggs that seem to get bigger every year!

As an avid recycler, once we have scoffed the contents, I reuse as much of the packaging I can...to create some spelling magic!

Creating some Easter egg spelling magic

The colourful card egg containers are perfect for cutting into flash cards, big enough to handle easily and write an 'ea' word on. It doesn't matter if the edges are uneven or curved, where the card formed the 'hole' into the box to reveal the egg inside. Unlike regular flash cards, which are uniform in size, the beauty of these is their irregularity and the different patterns on them. Their individuality will help your child to associate the spelling that is on them as they develop their photographic memory and visualising skills.

An obvious choice of spellings at Easter is to cover the 'ea' long vowel phoneme. You and your child could brainstorm words containing 'ea', in a spider diagram. Put 'ea' at the centre in an Easter egg shape, as a visual clue, then put 'ea' words

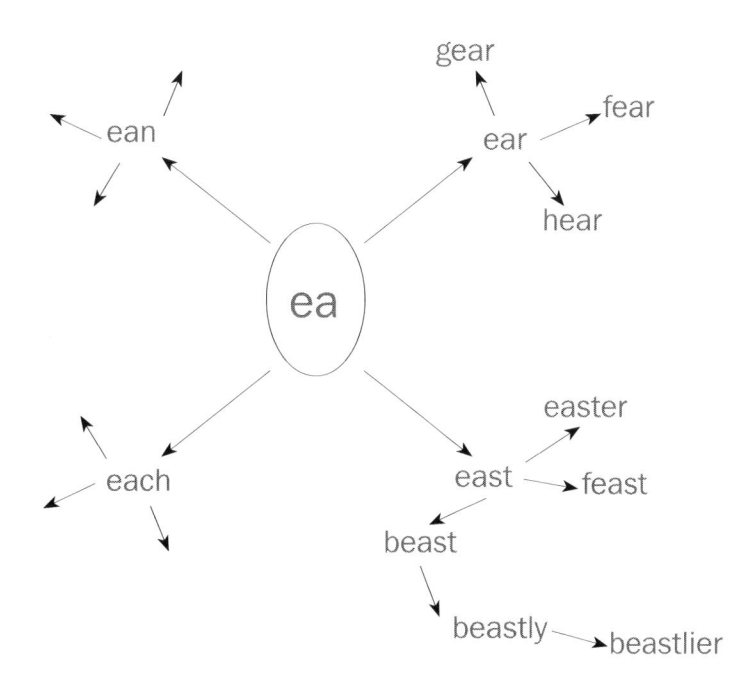

```
                    gear
                     ↑
         ean        ear → fear
          ↖         ↑
            ↖      hear
              ea
            ↙      ↘
         each       east → easter
                     ↓  ↘ feast
                   beast
                     ↓
                   beastly → beastlier
```

at the end of branches coming from the central image. From these words draw a handful of lines, at the end of which you can write an 'ea' word which rhymes with the parent word. (Illustration below)

If you get really engrossed in this activity you can keep adding branches and take the words one step further. So, for example, you may have 'east' on one of the first branches, then 'beast' coming from that, and 'beastly' growing out of that and 'beastlier' shooting from that!

These words can then be written on to a huge cut-out Easter egg or on lots of different coloured egg-shaped pieces of paper and stuck on a picture of a large Easter basket.

Or, you could have an Easter egg hunt with a difference! Draw a picture of a large chicken sitting on a nest or in a hen box. Under the chicken have a flap big enough to hide one of your egg-shaped 'ea' words. Take it in turns to choose an 'ea' egg to hide under the flap and the other players must guess which 'ea' egg is hidden.

And what about all the lovely, shiny, coloured foil the Easter eggs are wrapped up in? It would be such a waste to throw it away! Tear it into pieccs and then lightly scrunch it into pea-sized beads. These can then be threaded onto different lengths of string with a large needle, and be used like rosary beads, with each bead standing for a letter in a word your child is learning.

Some words have silent letters, such as 'know', 'through', 'white' and so on. It is helpful to have a string of beads with the same number of beads as letters in the word. If your child is trying to remember the spelling of 'white', they can make a string of five beads and move a bead along the string as they name or sound out the letters. Your child might even like to wear it as a bracelet as a prompt to practise the spelling; if your child is working on several words they could wear several bracelets and might even start a new craze!

Ed, a new friend for your younger child

If your child is at the stage of having to put 'doing' words into the past tense they have probably already met the 'ed' ending.

I like to personalise 'Ed' and make a life-size cut-out, as I did in chapter A for Al and Ally. Help your child to decorate Ed however they like – add a funny face, wool hair, colourful 'clothes' – to help them to engage in the activity. Encourage your child to look back through this chapter and underline all the verbs ending in 'ed' and then write them on Ed.

Now ask your child to find verbs in the present and write them out with 'ed' on them to put them into the past tense. With your help they will see that with a verb like 'move' they only need to add a 'd' as the word ends in 'e' anyway. They will also be or become aware of verbs like 'wear' that do not add 'ed' in the past tense. As you meet 'ed' endings in your reading and writing, add them to Ed.

You and your child can have fun making up interesting sentences about Ed, using some of the verbs you have collected, e.g. 'Ed hopped and skipped down the road, jumped across the bridge and dived into the river!'

Er

Another 'e' ending to words is the 'er' sound. While 'er' is the most common spelling, there are several others that make the same sound, including 'ir' (fir tree), 'ur' (murmur), 'ar' (collar), 'or' (doctor), 'our' (humour) and 're' (centre).

Get the green light for spelling with this traffic light activity

One way of approaching these different endings is to construct a set of traffic lights, with three large circles of paper in red, orange and green. (see photo below)

Because the spelling 'er' is the most common 'er' sound, label the green circle 'er'. To help with association (an accelerated learning tool) the orange circle can feature the next most common, 'or' words, and the red circle, less common 'ir' words. As you and your child come across words with these sounds write, type or stencil them out and stick them on the appropriate traffic light.

Once your child is familiar with the different traffic light sounds, you can add traffic signs for 'ar' and 'ur' words and the warning triangles for the more complicated 'our' and 're' endings. This makes quite a striking display and has the added advantage of incorporating some valuable road safety knowledge!

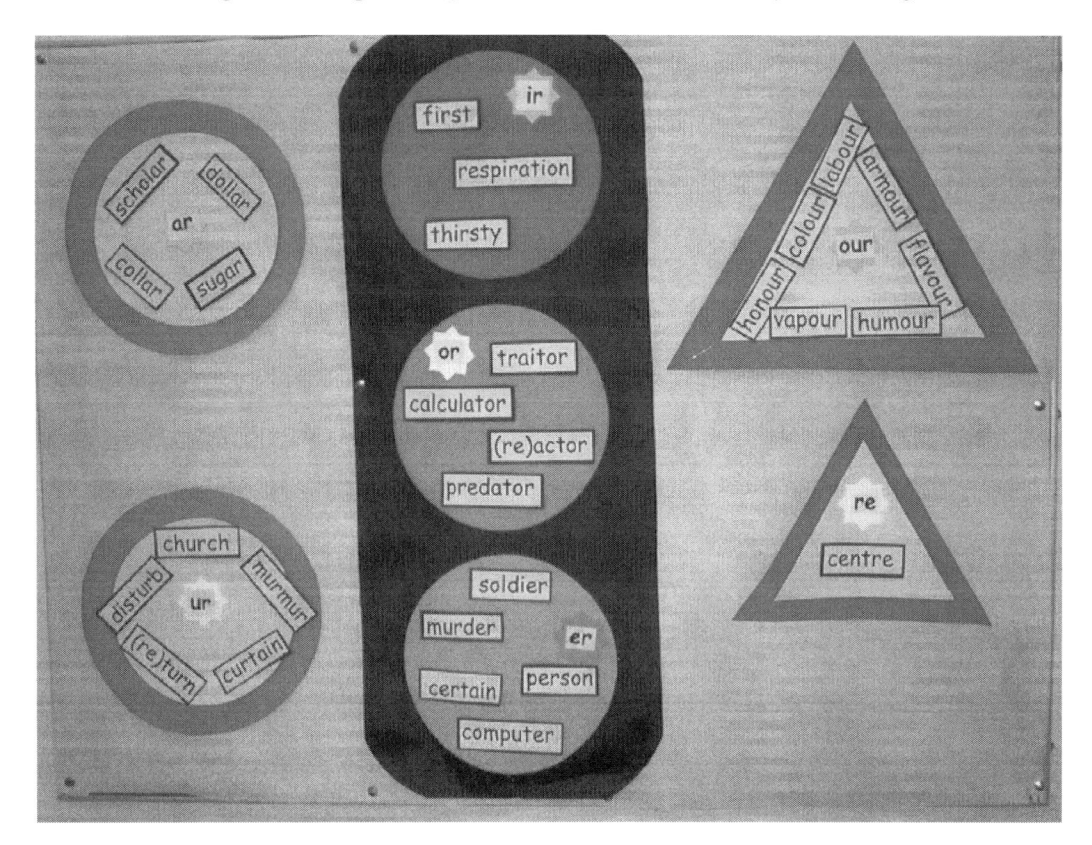

'Enry the enormous mouse

You may have thought from the title of this chapter that the size of 'Enry the Enormous Mouse was because he had eaten all the Easter eggs! Thankfully, this is not the case. In fact, the mouse is enormous because it actually helps to teach some advanced spelling – the 'ous' ending.

First of all, the mouse is called 'Enry, not because of laziness in pronunciation, but to help children remember that the word 'enormous', which is often pronounced 'inormous', actually begins with an 'e'.

The 'ous' ending is pronounced 'us', with a short vowel sound, whereas in the word 'mouse' the 'magic e' has been added to change the vowel into a long vowel sound. Positioning 'mouse' alongside 'enormous' seems to help children to remember the 'mous' ending.

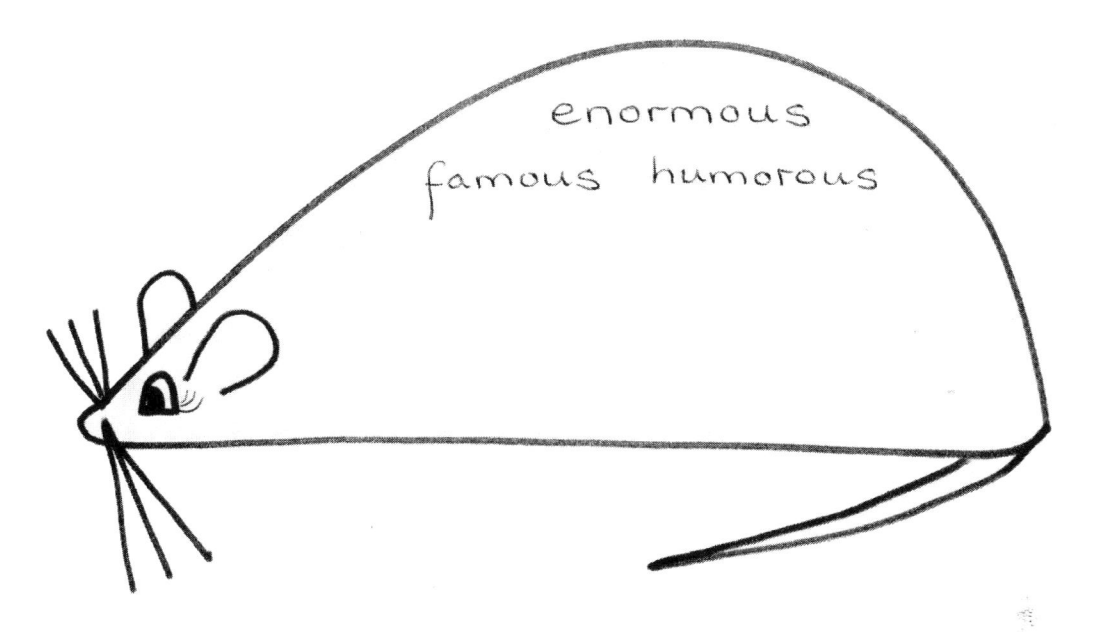

[Drawing of a mouse with the words "enormous", "famous", "humorous" written on its body]

I am by no stretch of the imagination an artist but children seem to like my picture of 'Enry, even though I give him such long, curling eyelashes that he should probably be called 'Enrietta! Your child could probably draw a much better mouse, big enough to accommodate all the 'ous' words you will be able to find together.

An 'e' homophone: effect /affect

Both of these words are verbs, but 'effect' is usually used as a noun, preceded by 'the'. So a useful way to remember the difference is to talk about 'the effect of global warming on the planet' (with the two e's together) or 'global warming affects the planet.'

An 'e' word to syllabify : e/vap/or/a/tion

This is an appropriate word to suggest, following our work on the 'er' sound. Here, the sound is spelt 'or'.

My method for helping children to remember is to tell them to think of the delicious image of pouring delicious evaporated milk onto jelly.

An 'e' mnemonic: 'pretty' and 'quiet'

Ask your child to draw or copy a picture of that most famous of aliens, ET, and then write underneath: ET is pretty quiet.

The magic 'e' rule

It is important to understand long and short vowels, (see 'Coding vowels' in Chapter C) before introducing 'magic e'.

The reason 'e' is magic is that it has the power to change a short vowel into a long vowel. So, 'mat' changes to 'mate' when magic e is added, 'can' changes to 'cane', 'pin' to 'pine' and so on.

Magic e

It isn't fashionable to talk about the 'magic e' nowadays, but I think it sounds a lot more fun than 'vowel, consonant e'.

Make a magic wand for magic e

Your daughter or son would probably love to make a magic witch or wizard's wand with a silver star at the end with an 'e' stuck on it. Encourage them to be as creative as possible and decorate their magic wand with streamers, ribbons and glitter.

Then your child can compile a list of cvc words (consonant, vowel, consonant) where the vowel is short, write them on cards and code them with a smile (macron – see 'Coding vowels in chapter C).

And now for the magic bit...your child taps each card with her magic wand, writes the new word with the 'magic e' at the end on a different card and codes the new word with a line (breve – again, see 'Coding vowels' in chapter C). These cards can be used to play even more spelling games such as pairs, snap or even dominoes.

To make the difference when using the 'magic e' more visually apparent and memorable, your child could draw pictures on the cards so that a pin is seen to change to a pine tree, a cap to a cape and so on.

'Magic e' affects lots of words, not just cvc words, as we shall find out in further chapters.

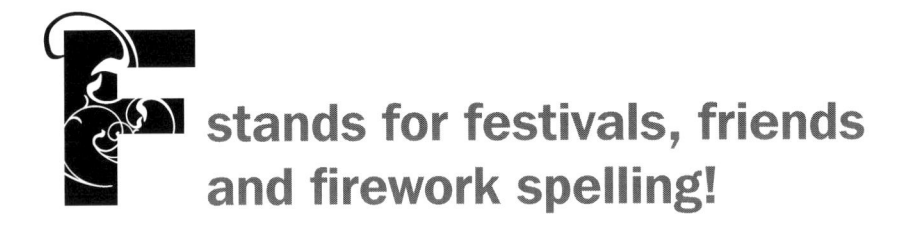

F stands for festivals, friends and firework spelling!

Extra materials needed:

- Paint charts from your local DIY store
- Pearlised nail varnish
- Glitter glue

We have already enjoyed some activities around the Christian festivals of Christmas and Easter but with so many other cultures and religions around us your child will benefit from knowing about the festivals of other religions. Many of them have wonderful, polysyllabic names that will extend your child's reading skills, as they split the words into chunks to read them.

The spelling of the festival names, however, may cause confusion as they differ from the conventions of English spelling. Many of the Hindu and Sikh festivals end in ' i ' whereas no English word ends in ' i '. (See chapter I). The spelling of Islamic festivals includes the letter 'q' on its own, whereas in English 'q' is always accompanied by 'u' and the festival Hajj is spelt with a double 'j', whereas no English word ends in a 'j'.

Celebrate spelling with fabulously colourful festivals

However, the meanings of the festivals are rich with possibilities. The Sikh celebration Diwali, like the Jewish Hannukah, is a festival of lights, so you and your child could explore the background to this and do some spelling work on 'light'. (See the next chapter for ideas on the 'ght' sound). Perhaps you could make a lantern template and cut out lots of lights and put an 'ight' word in each one.

The Hindu celebration Holi is the coloured water spring festival, so perhaps your child could learn the spellings of all the colours, with raindrop shaped pieces of paper coloured according to the spelling featured. Extend your child's vocabulary and spelling bank by thinking of different terms for blue - for example turquoise, navy, aquamarine, harebell blue - and group all your different shades of blue raindrops together.

Then repeat the exercise with all the variant shades of red – crimson, cherry, vermilion, magenta and so on – and carry on until you have covered all the colours. You should end up with an attractive fountain or rainbow display as the colour families merge into each other.

Paint charts from your local DIY store will help your child to appreciate the vast range of colours available and you could cut mosaic tiles from them and stick them on to your raindrops until the raindrop is covered with little pieces of that colour. Experiment with applying a wash of diluted PVA glue or a coat or an outline of clear or pearlised nail varnish to give a wonderfully watery sheen or shimmer!

Spelling with friends

Two new friends to introduce to your younger child who is beginning to write sentences are Fatty Freddy and Chubby Charlie. They are great friends to have as they help your child remember full stops and capital letters. Fatty Freddy is the round full stop and wherever Fatty Freddy goes, Chubby Charlie, the big capital letter, will follow – at the beginning of the next sentence.

A fun way of helping your child to understand the need for punctuation is to try to read the following in one breath!

'Astronauts float in space rice pudding is my favourite sweet boys play football after school in the bath I play with a rubber duck under my bed I hide my pocket money all over the cake were scattered chocolate buttons Christmas trees look lovely when lit up with a great bang the bomb exploded high up on the tightrope the girl walked carefully in case it rains we shall take umbrellas with us to prevent the cat scratching us we will have to cut its claws unless it stops thundering we will stay indoors.'

Well done, if you manage it! At first sight, the passage looks as though it is one, long nonsensical sentence. It is, in fact, a collection of 12 sentences that need separating with full stops. Each sentence needs, of course, to start with a capital letter. As an extra exercise, see if your child can find the sentences and insert the correct punctuation.

Young children like the idea of talking about Fatty Freddy followed by Chubby Charlie, but be careful that they do not try to write out laboriously 'F-a-t-t-y F-r-e-d-d-y' at the end of a sentence instead of using a full stop, as one of my first pupils did!

Some mnemonics for 'friend':

There are several ways to help with the spelling of this word. I like the phrase 'I to the end will be your friend' as it has a simple, memorable rhyme and helps your child remember to put an ' i ' next to the 'end'.

You could also say 'Friday is the end of the week' and teach your child to put 'fri' and 'end' together to spell 'friend'.

Other children like to visualise a huge frying pan with a group of friends lying in it and think of 'fried friends'!

Finger spelling

This technique can also help with the spelling of 'friend'. It has a silent ' i ' so your child may be tempted to sound out the word as 'f-r-e-n-d'.

Hold up six fingers and as your child says each letter put down a finger. If he gets to the end and there is a finger left he will realise there is another letter. It may also help to stress the silent ' i ' as he says it. Finger spelling is particularly helpful when there are silent letters, as a reminder to think carefully what the silent letter is.

Flossy words

These are words with a short vowel that end in 'f', 'l', 's' or 'z' double the final consonant, for example fluff, will, kiss, buzz.

Of course, there are always exceptions to the rule! There are two common 2-letter exceptions, 'if' and 'of' and three 3- letter exceptions, 'yes', 'gas' and 'pal' and a common 4- letter example, 'this'.

Your child might like to see how many words they can make using the flossy rule. Fold a piece of A4 paper, laid horizontally on the table, in half and then into quarters (a sneaky bit of maths thrown in there!), so that the paper is divided into four columns.

In the first column, write in big letters some letters and initial consonant blends, such as: b, d, f, k, s, t, ch, st, sn, & fl.

In the second column, write the five short vowel sounds: a e i o u.

In the third column, write: ff, ll, ss, zz

In the fourth column, write possible endings or suffixes, such as: y, ed & ing.

Now, take a letter or blend from each column and try to make a flossy word.

It's a good idea to start with a certain consonant from the first column, choose a double consonant from the third column and go through the vowels in order to see if you can make words from those combinations first. Then, keep the same initial consonant but change the double consonant and work through the vowels again. Only when you have got a good list using the first three columns, start adding the suffixes from the fourth column.

You could have a family competition and see who in the course of a week can come up with the most flossy words and give a prize to the winner! It will undoubtedly extend your child's spelling vocabulary and it would be affirming to work as a family on the same project.

An 'f' word to syllabify: fun/da/men/tal

This would be a good to time to revise the 'al' suffix or ending and you could add the words 'fundamental' and 'fundamentally' to Al and Ally (see Chapter A). Make sure your child knows what 'fundamental' means, perhaps by looking it up in a dictionary, and that they can use it confidently in sentences.

An 'f' rule:

'Full' is an example of a flossy word, but when it is used at the beginning or the end of a word it is spelt with just one 'l'. For example:

Beautiful, helpful, useful, fulsome, fulfil.

However, be careful that your child does not think of 'full moon' as one word or words such as 'full time', 'full scale' or 'full-back', which are sometimes hyphenated to join two words together.

'F' homophones : feat /feet flour /flower and fare /fair

1. Feat/feet

'Feat' is not a very commonly used word in a youngster's vocabulary but if you want to teach it to them, you could explain the meaning and give an example of its use, as well as giving them clues to the spelling, in the following sentence:

'It would be a tremendous feat to eat all that meat!'

In a similar way, group some 'ee' words in the same sentence to help spell 'feet'.

'You can see your feet below your knees.'

2. Flour/flower

I'm surprised no bakery has yet adopted the slogan 'Our flour makes the best bread' or perhaps it has and I just don't know about it! Either way, it could help iron out the confusion between 'flour' and 'flower'.

As a child of the 60s, I always think of 'flower power', so I visualise those spellings together. Introduce your child to the hippy era and flower power. They may like to draw a flower around both the 'o' letters to anchor the image.

3. Fare/fair

Show your child the play on words in the following statement:

You won't go far if you don't pay the fare.

Then suggest your child may like to draw a picture of a girl with fair hair at a fairground to help them remember 'fair'. If your child is a good artist they may like to draw a picture of a child looking upset because they are not tall enough to go on a certain ride while saying 'It's not fair!' in a little speech bubble above their head.

Firework spelling

Another way to remember the spelling of 'fair' is to put 'fair' in the centre of a firework or spelling sparkler (see Chapter B). Then have other words sparking out from the centre. Your child could decorate it with coloured crayon sparks or coloured glitter glue to make it sparkle.

```
       air      hair
         \    /
  pair — fair — chair
         /    \
       lair    stair
```

G stands for gingerbread, gnomes and glitter

Extra materials needed:

• Tray (a new cat litter tray or a kitchen tray with raised sides are ideal)

• Sandpit sand or cooking salt

• Glitter

• Gingerbread dough

Glitter tray game

Glitter trays are a variation on sand trays that young children can write in when they are learning the shape and 'feel' of letters. Sand trays can easily be made at home from a new cat litter tray filled with sandpit sand. The sand feels cool to the touch and enhances the feel of the letters as the child writes the letter shapes with a finger.

An alternative to sand is cooking salt and this can be dressed up with seasonal silver glitter for Christmas, to look like snow! While it looks prettier than sand, it does tend to be a little scratchy and some children prefer the smoothness of sand to salt.

Either medium offers a multi-sensory approach to learning letters that particularly benefits dyslexic children, who need to use as many senses as possible when learning, but also enhances and accelerates learning for any youngster.

SPELLING MADE MAGIC – An A-Z of spelling tips and tricks

Gimme, gimme

If your child is still enjoying making an alphabet arc at the beginning of their spelling sessions, you could play the game 'Gimme, gimme' with them. Once they have put the arc together correctly and have recited the alphabet, pointing to the letters as they name them, they are ready to play.

If your child is at the earliest stage of learning the letter names and sounds, you could say to them 'Gimme a 'duh'(d) and they find the letter and put it in the centre of the space under the arc. You then ask them, 'What does it say?' They should reply with the name of the letter – 'dee'. They then replace the letter in the correct place in the arc and you repeat the procedure with a different letter.

Once they have got the hang of this, you can keep the letters in the space until you have got three, four or five letters waiting to go back in the arc. When you ask your child to replace them in the arc this will test their alphabetic knowledge as to whether they can put the letters back in the correct place.

An amusing variant to this spelling game is to reverse the roles, so that your child says to you, 'Gimme' a range of letters. When it is your turn to replace the letters in the arc, deliberately misplace one or two. Your child will love to check that you have done this correctly and will pounce on any 'errors' with glee! Putting them in the role of 'teacher' is a wonderful way to consolidate their knowledge, without them even realising.

If your child is learning to blend or crash letters together, you can extend the activity and say, 'Gimme a 'suh' (s) …. Gimme a 'huh' (h)…..What does that spell?' Your child should reply 'Sh.' You could then brainstorm words that begin with the 'sh' sound and end with the sound. Words that end in the same sound clearly rhyme, so it is easy to build up a list of words with the same ending e.g. dish, fish and wish.

Gradually, you can use 'Gimme, gimme' to spell simple words. You might say, 'Gimme a 'cuh' (c)....Gimme a 'huh' (h)....What does that spell?' Reply: 'Ch'.
' Now gimme an 'o'...Gimme a 'p'...What does that spell?'
Reply: 'Chop'
By asking your child to exchange letters, you can make new words. For example, you might say:

'Change the 'o' for an 'a'....What does that spell?'
Reply: 'Chap.'

'Change the 'a' for an 'i'. What does that spell?'
'Chip.'

'Change the 'c' for a 's'. What does that spell?'
'Ship.'

'Change the 'h' to a 'l'. What does that spell?'
'Slip.'

'Change the 'p' to a 'm'. What does that spell?'
'Slim.'

It will really make your child think about the spelling of words if you reverse roles and they have to talk you through the changes of letters!

Hard and soft 'g'

Depending on the vowel that follows it, 'g' can sound hard or soft.

If it is followed by 'a', 'o' or 'u' it sounds hard, as in 'gate', 'got' or 'gun'.

When followed by an 'e', an 'i' or the 'half vowel' 'y' it usually sounds soft, as in 'gem', 'gin' or 'gypsy'.

Of course, there will always be exceptions – such as 'get'.

Gingerbread letters

The word 'ginger' is a useful memory word as it has the soft 'g' with both the 'e' and the 'i'. It also gives us an excuse to do a little baking again and make some gingerbread letters to make soft 'g' words! You may remember that when we discussed eating our words in Chapter B, I warned you that using chocolate dough for letters would prompt fits of giggles. I'm afraid that gingerbread dough looks just as bad, but no doubt the hilarity involved in the exercise will help your children remember the soft 'g' rule!

I find it is easier to fashion letters from rolled sausages of dough than to try to cut round letter shapes. As a preparatory exercise, your child might like to look in the dictionary and see which words begin with 'ge' or 'gi' and write them down. A number of words end in 'ge' and 'gy', such as 'orange', 'garage' and 'energy'. Once your child has amassed a list of soft 'g' words, you can make plenty of gingerbread letters, so that when they are cooked you can use them to make words and enjoy some edible spelling!

Gnome words

As well as soft 'g' words there are also some silent 'g' words. Younger children will probably have come across these words where the 'g' sound is silent:

gnome   gnaw   gnash   gnashers   gnat   gnarled

Your child might remember these words if they were put into one sentence thus:

The gnat gnawed at the gnarled tree while the gnome gnashed his gnashers. Or, they could colour in a gnome figure and stick silent 'g' words on to or around the picture to help them visualise the spellings.

Older children may have come across the words:

Gnocchi   reign   campaign   sign   design   neighbour

Perhaps they could look out for other silent 'g' words and make up their own sentence or poem using them all.

The 'ght' words

A collection of 'gnome words' that need dealing with on their own are those that feature the 'ght' sound. This is a really difficult cluster of letters to master, as it has two silent letters, the 'g' and the 'h'. Children often put the 't' and the 'h' together, as in 'th', because they are familiar with the 'th' sound. Remind your child that the letters appear in alphabetical order so the 'h' comes before the 't'.

Lightbulb game

Lots of practice is required for writing out 'ght' words. Your child could make a poster featuring a huge light bulb with a collection of 'ight' words inside. Using these rhyming words they could write a poem. For example, they could write a poem about Bonfire Night, when fireworks brighten the sky with light and the bonfire and guy are set alight.

A 'g' acrostic : right

This acrostic might also help your child remember the 'ght' spelling.

Ride **I**n **G**ranny's **H**elicopter **T**onight
And then you'll get the spelling right!

Of course, you may prefer to devise your own memorable acrostic. It is fun to play around with words and conjure up images that stick in the mind and cement the spelling in the memory.

A 'g' word to syllabify: gi/gan/tic

A 'g' homophone: great/grate

If your child is a good artist, ask them to draw a picture of a rat grating cheese onto his supper, so that they remember the 'rat' in 'grate'.

For 'great', think of a way of associating the word with 'eat' and 'meat'. It could be the sentence 'It is great to eat meat' or your child could draw and label a picture of Alexander the Great eating a huge plateful of meat! Let your creativity run riot!

H is for Harry Potter!

Extra materials needed:

You don't need any extra materials for this chapter.

One of the trickiest rules for youngsters to master is the doubling rule – but surprisingly it's Harry Potter who has saved the day!

The doubling rule is that when you add an ending beginning with a vowel to a one syllable word with one short vowel you must double the final consonant. This is to prevent the newly added vowel changing the first vowel, in the same way as 'magic e' does.

It is sometimes known as the 111 rule, (one syllable, one short vowel and one final consonant), but children also respond to it as the 'double glazing rule'. One vowel at the end of the word is not strong enough to keep out the effect of a vowel being added. So we have to put in double glazing by doubling the consonant.

For example, to keep the 'o' short in 'hop' when we put it into the past tense, we must double the 'p' or else 'magic e' will make the vowel change into a long vowel, resulting in 'hoped' instead of 'hopped'. In the same way, if we wanted to add 'ing' to 'hop', we would have to double the 'p' or the word would become 'hoping', which has an entirely different meaning from 'hopping'! This is because the vowel at the beginning of any suffix will change the preceding vowel – not just 'magic e'.

Harry Potter is a perfect example to use to help your child remember this rule. If we did not double the consonants in his name, he would be called 'Ha(i)ry Poter', which simply does not have the same appeal!

Doubling rule game

Fold a piece of paper into six columns. Leave the first column blank and then at the top of the next five columns write 'add ing', 'add ed', 'add er' 'add y' and 'add age'.

In the first column write your choice of 1-syllable words with a short vowel, for example, skip, cut, run, stop, kit, rib, cot (not every word will go with each ending). I have included 'cot' so that your child can understand why 'cottage' has the double 't'. They may like to code the vowels again as we did in chapter C and E, with a smile to indicate the short vowel.

Happiness!

Everyone wants to be happy! I like to teach my pupils this little song, that you may recognise, because it is an excellent aid to spelling and also illustrates the doubling rule.

I'm h-a-p-p-y!
I am h-a-p-p-y!
I know I am, I'm sure I am,
I'm h-a-p-p-y!

The root word is 'hap', which we don't use in that form, although we use the word 'perhaps' and talk about a 'mishap'. When we add an ending beginning in a vowel (and remember that 'y' is considered a half vowel), we need to double the consonant.

Once your child can spell 'happy', perhaps with the aid of the song, you can ask them to play the 'Change' game. This is the same game we played after 'Gimme, gimme' in the last chapter, when you change one letter in a word to give a new word.

As an example, you could ask your child to change the 'a' to an 'i' and ask them what that spells. Correct reply: 'hippy'. Then change the 'p' (both of them) to a 'l', giving you 'hilly'. Then you could change the 'h' to a 's' to give 'silly' and so on. If you and your child fancy a timed challenge, see how many changes you can each write down in so many minutes and compare notes. If you are feeling particularly clever, you might like to bring the changes full circle so that you eventually come back to the word with which you started!

A 'h' homophone: hear/here

A useful memory aid is to construct the 'Words of place' triangle, as it helps with the spelling of the three main words of place – 'here', 'there' and 'where' and distinguishes them from their homophones ('hear', 'their' and 'wear').

Ask your child to write out the word 'here' seven times in a column, in a favourite colour. Then, in a different colour, add a 't' to the second 'here' to make 'there'. Now, in a different colour again, add a 'w' to the remaining 'here' to make 'where'.

The difference in colours should highlight the fact that all the words of place contain the root word 'here'. Now, in front of the last 4 'where' words, add these prefixes in turn: 'no', 'any', 'some' and 'every'. You should be able to slip in a little Maths and construct a right angled triangle around all the words to do with 'place'.

here

there

where

no**w**here

any**w**here

some**w**here

every**w**here

An easy way to distinguish between 'here' and 'hear' is to think 'You hear with your ear.'

Heel/heal

The easiest way to differentiate between these is to link 'heel' with 'feet' and also 'knee', so that the three parts of the leg contain the double 'ee'.

Hour/our

A little French lesson could be useful here. In French the clock is known as 'une horloge', (pronounced 'oon orlozh'), with a silent 'h'. An hour is known as 'une heure' ('oon ur') again with a silent 'h'. The English 'hour' also has a silent 'h'. Thus, the word that is the unit of time begins with a silent 'h'.

The word for 'belonging to us' replaces each word with one letter so is simply the 3-letter word 'our'.

More silent 'h' words: honest, honour and heir

In her book, 'How to Manage and Detect Dyslexia', Philomena Ott gives a useful mnemonic for these silent 'h' words:

It will be an honour to meet the honest heir in an hour's time.

Homonyms/homophones

Each chapter we look at homophones (literally, 'same sound') – words that sound the same, but are spelt differently. There are some words that do the opposite and are called 'homonyms' (literally, 'same name') because they are spelt the same but have different meanings. The word 'lead' is an example because it can be the name of a soft metal, something you attach to a dog's collar when walking the dog or the doing word 'to lead someone to safety'.

You and your child may like to think of as many homonyms as you can. Here are some to start you off: left, leaves, read, rock, quiver, wind.

I am always amused when I read that the Centre for the Teaching of Reading is in Reading! Is it coincidental, I wonder?

A 'h' word to syllabify: har/mo/ni/ous

This is another word to add to 'Enry the enormous mouse (from chapter E). You could also ask your child what the 'root' word is (harmony) and if they remember why the 'y' has been changed to an 'i' (see Chapter C).

A tricky 'h' word to visualise: half

This is one of those words where it is tempting to suggest to your child that they pronounce the word as it is written, sounding the 'l' so that it rhymes with Alf! They might like to draw a picture of a big man eating half of an enormous pizza, with the caption 'Alf ate half the pizza!'

Hangman

A great way to start or end a spelling session is to play a game of hangman, using one of the words covered in that lesson or the preceding one. This helps you revise and consolidate difficult words or introduce new words. Your child will love to think of some obscure word to ensure that it's you that gets hung! 'Gypsy' is always a good word to choose as usually players go through all the vowels, confidently expecting to fill at least one space with a letter. It is a useful reminder that 'y' is a half-vowel!

I stands for Magic Ian

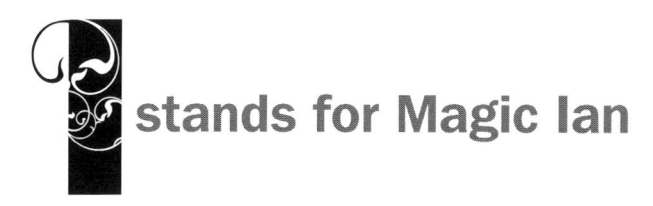

Extra materials needed:

• Computer and printer (for typing out letters in different fonts and printing)

• String

No, Magic Ian is not some relative of Harry Potter that JK Rowling forgot to mention, but a new addition to your classroom clan that so far comprises Al, Ally and Ed. So, get that leftover roll of wallpaper out and draw round your child again to make a life-size cut-out of Ian.

In chapter C we mentioned the 'tion' suffix in the context of syllabification. Once your child has mastered the art of chopping long words into chunks and learnt the 'tion' suffix, the spelling of hundreds of words is at their fingertips…'addition', 'subtraction', 'multiplication', 'magition'…. Oops. 'Magition?' No, that's not right. What's wrong?

Magic Ian to the rescue! A person with the 'ion' ending is actually spelt 'ian', So Magic Ian is a magician, Electric Ian is an electrician and so on. My electrician is actually called Ian and that gave me the idea of separating his name from his specialism. Ask your child to find the careers of these Ians!

Music Ian   Mathematic Ian   Statistic Ian   Politic(s) Ian

The specialism has to end in 'c' to blend with 'Ian'. In the case of Politic(s) Ian, we simply leave out the 's'. With a little spelling magic, Beauty Ian becomes Beautic Ian or beautician. There we applied the rule from Chapter C – 'Change the y to an i when you add an ending'.

Your child can do the same for History Ian, but because they will end up with two i's together delete the superfluous one. How about Theology Ian. You now have nine Ians to stencil, print or write out on to slips of paper or jigcards (perhaps separating the specialism from the name 'Ian') that you can stick on your life-size Ian. Your challenge is to find a tenth Ian!

An 'i' rule: No English word ends in an 'i'.

There is bound to be an exception to this rule, but when your child says, "What about 'spaghetti'?", remind them that 'spaghetti' is an Italian word. 'Taxi' is short for 'taxicab' and names like 'Judi' and 'Vicki' are also short forms of longer names. Nowadays, it is trendy to end names in 'i', like 'Aimi', but strictly speaking this is derived from 'Amy' or 'Aimee'. In general, English vocabulary will not end in an 'i'.

A polysyllabic word: re/spon/si/bi/li/ty

This is a lovely word to syllabify, with all those two letter 'i' syllables. It sounds as though there should be four 'i's, but because no English word ends in an 'i' we change the last 'i' sound into a 'y'.

Once your child has mastered chopping the word into its six syllables (a good tip is to try putting their hand under their chin to 'feel' the syllables as the jaw moves) and spelling them out, you could ask them how to spell the plural form of the word. This will enable you to see if they have remembered the C rule we mentioned earlier and covered in Chapter C – 'Change the y to an i when you add an ending'. Thus, your child should spell it 'responsibilities'.

If they omit the final 'e', just tell them that if the word ended in 'is' it would sound like 'iss' (as in 'axis' or 'osmosis') so we add an 'e' to make it sound right. Look ahead to chapter Y if your child wants to discuss this more.

Another 'i' rule: When spelling the 'e' sound, it is 'i' before 'e' except after 'c'.

This is a well-known rule but is worth mentioning here as it helps us spell such tricky words as 'receive'. A couple of exceptions to the rule are 'seize' and 'protein'.

Give your older child a challenge to see how many 'cei' words they can record as they come across them in the week ahead.

An 'i' homophone: its/it's

This is a confusing homophone because it seems to contradict the rule of belonging. When something belongs to someone, we use an apostrophe to indicate that, as in 'Simon's book', 'Tamsin's dress' or 'Chloe's room'. Therefore, children often put an apostrophe after 'it' when something belongs to 'it'. E.g. 'The cat has hurt it's paw.' But this is not correct.

When we say, "It's yours!" or "It's theirs!" or "It's ours!" we don't use an apostrophe before the 's' in 'yours', 'theirs' or 'ours', so we don't with 'its' either. What you will be able to see from the above is that we DO use the apostrophe when we shorten or contract 'It is' to 'it's', to show that we have missed out a letter.

Ask your child to insert apostrophes where appropriate in the following:

Its raining.	Its wing	Its tail	Its hail
Its eyes	its hot	its not	its nose

(The apostrophes should go in the following: 'It's raining', 'It's hail', 'It's hot' and 'It's not'.)

Other 'I' contractions

There are several 'I' contractions such as 'I'm', 'I'd', 'I'll' and 'I've'. These are small words that can be difficult to differentiate, particularly for dyslexic youngsters who associate pictures with words. If they read the word 'horse' they see a horse in their mind's eye and if they read the very similar word 'house' they can distinguish it from 'horse' because they get a mental picture of a house. But what picture does the word 'I'd' conjure up? Exactly, nothing!

This is why it is the little words like 'the', 'then', that' or 'with' that dyslexics find so troublesome. They may be able to syllabify, picture and read 'Ty/ran/no/saur/us Rex' but stumble on the word 'they'.

To help your child, whether they are dyslexic or not, to distinguish between the different 'I' contractions, make a Pairs game by typing out these contractions in different fonts and colours and sticking them on to cards to match up. (For dyslexic children or those with visual discrimination difficulties, who find this game troublesome, look ahead to Chapter P for a possible solution.)

I'm	I'd	I'll	I've	it's	it'll	it'd

I suggest using different colours and fonts so that your child will not necessarily be pairing up the same colours or fonts, which makes the activity more challenging. It will also serve to challenge their (and your!) powers of memory.

An 'i' word to syllabify: in/ter/est/ing

This word can catch youngsters out, as it is often pronounced 'intresting' with the first 'e' omitted. It can be helpful to enunciate the syllables slowly, as heard in some spy or war films, "Ve-ry in-ter-est-ing!"

Silent 'i' words

We have already mentioned some words that contain a silent 'i', including 'business' and 'marriage' in Chapter C, with the rule 'Change the 'y' to an 'i' when you add an ending'.

Another word with a silent 'i' is the tricky word 'parliament'. An easy way to remember the silent 'i' in the word is to think of the phrase 'I am in parliament' or 'Liam is in parliament.'

The 'ir' blend

In Chapter E we looked at the 'er' sound which has many forms, including the less common 'ir' form. When spelling such words as 'girl' and 'bird' children tend to want to write 'ri', probably because they are so used to writing 'r' as the second letter in such consonant blends as 'br', 'cr', 'dr' and so on. However, if you ask your child if a certain male celebrity or footballer is going out with a 'girl' or a 'grill' they will find the question funny and the correct spelling more memorable!

The following visual aid may help your child to visualise the 'ir' spelling. A rosette for first place is positioned in the word 'first' so that the 1 becomes the 'i'.

SPELLING MADE MAGIC – An A-Z of spelling tips and tricks

It is worth spending some time focusing on 'ir' and encouraging your child to write 'ir' several times, joining the 'i' to the 'r', so that they appreciate the 'feel' of the letters flowing into each other. Then you could ask them to construct words around the 'ir'.

A tricky word: island

An easy way to remember this spelling with its silent 's' is to think:

An island is land surrounded by water!

A long 'i' activity

In Chapter E we covered 'magic e'. Your child should now be aware that 'magic e' makes 'Tim' say 'time' and 'kit' say 'kite'. Why not make some long 'I' kites, as in the picture below, and have a little fun making a beautiful display to go on the wall, featuring lots of long 'i' words.

J is for Jack, Jake and Jolly Jelly

Extra materials needed:

Fudge (buy soft fudge or make your own)

If you look at the letter 'c', it is round and robust and is quite a 'strong' letter. By comparison, the letter 'k' looks quite spindly and not very steady on its feet, like a giraffe! Perhaps this is why whenever a 'k' follows a vowel it needs some support, whether it is from a consonant like 'c' or from 'magic e'.

Children often get confused with the 'c' sound. In the next chapter we shall learn how to decide whether a word starts with a 'kicky k' or a 'curly c'.

At the end of a word of one syllable and one vowel the 'c' sound is provided by either 'ck' or 'ke', depending on whether the vowel is short or long. It is crucial to pick the right one or the meaning of your sentence could be radically changed. I once had a pupil who wrote, "I lick snakes"! I knew that he kept snakes for a hobby so I was sure he meant "I like snakes." However, he could just as easily have intended to write "I like snacks!"

The names Jack and Jake illustrate the difference clearly. Jack has a short vowel so takes the 'ck' ending. As we know from Chapter E, 'magic e' makes the vowel go long – as in the case of Jake. Ask your child to draw a picture of a boy called Jack, who might have a pack on his back, and mount it on black card. Then draw a picture of a boy called Jake eating a cake by a lake and mount it on a different colour card.

SPELLING MADE MAGIC – An A-Z of spelling tips and tricks

Now, divide the following words into team Jack or team Jake, depending on whether they are 'ck' words or 'ke' words. It would be good to write them down and code them according to whether they have a short vowel (coded with a smile above the vowel) or a long vowel (a line above the vowel). This makes the pattern clear and reinforces the earlier teaching about long and short vowels.

joke stack lick bloke Mick quake block Blake trick stock duke quack Jock Mike duck stake black snake back trike stoke like snack bake

Then ask your child to hold the pictures of Jack and Jake, one in each hand, while you call out one of the words from the list. Your child must hold up the right team leader – Jack or Jake. Ideally, this should be played with more than one player so that the winner of each round is the first person to hold up the correct card. Each player must draw their own picture cards of Jack and Jake or your child may like to produce several which can be used by other members of the family or visiting friends. Keep a tally of who wins each point (another sneaky bit of Maths) and the winner of the game is the person with the most points.

Another activity involves mounting all the words on cards and playing a Pairs game – pairing up 'block' with 'bloke', 'Mick' with 'Mike' and so on. Each player must read the words aloud as they pick them and must read a pair correctly to keep it.

The 'j' rule: No English word ends in a 'j'

Lots of words sound as though they end in a 'j' sound but in English the 'j' sound is made with 'dge' or 'ge'.

Words with a short vowel use 'dge':

ba**dge**r, e**dge**, bri**dge**, lo**dge**r, fu**dge**

Words with a long vowel sound use 'ge' :

a**ge**, hu**ge**, Ni**ge**l

Words with a consonant before the 'j' sound use 'ge':

lar**ge**, hin**ge**, bul**ge**

Words with two vowels making one sound use 'ge':

Scroo**ge**, gau**ge**

Ask your child to put the correct 'j' sound to complete these words:

ba	sl	bar	ra
Mi	hu	ju	le
bul	hin	sta	gun

Encourage them to say each word with a long and then a short vowel sound to help develop their auditory discrimination, so that they 'hear' which is the correct choice of 'j' sound.

A fun activity with fudge

This is another way to get your children eating their words! Have a cookery lesson involving practical Maths and Science (all that weighing and measuring) and make a batch of fudge. Careful – it gets extremely hot! Once your fudge is cool enough to handle, you and your child can fashion it into letters by rolling balls of fudge into sausages which can then be shaped into letters. See how many words you can make with fudge using the 'dge' sound. To qualify for the reward of eating a fudge letter your child must remember which 'j' sound is used by one of the words in the assorted list above!

Jig-cards

I am a big fan of using jig-cards – cards bearing segments or syllables of words to be put together to make long words. We have already used them on Al and Ally, Ed and Ian, but you may like to take the examples of polysyllabic spelling we have included in each chapter and make jig-cards of the syllables. Then you could muddle them up and your child could sort them and position them to make the long word. This would be useful revision and is a lovely introductory or final activity in a spelling session – particularly if you time how long it takes your child to complete the task and see if they can beat their time in the next lesson!

Or, if you have two children doing this, with a matching set of jig-cards each, you can have a competition to see who completes all the jig-cards first! Children love the competitive element. Make sure they can read the words they have compiled and know their meanings.

Another activity with jig-cards that adds some extra fun is to make up new words by putting different syllables together and reading the new 'nonsense' words. This is invaluable for improving reading skills, because the reader cannot guess the word but must carefully decode it, breaking it down into chunks. This will really boost your child's confidence about tackling unknown, long words in their reading and will improve their competence.

The Jolly Jelly game

We played a version of this in Chapter H but it's refreshing to revisit activities in slightly different formats. The idea is to start a chain of words beginning with jolly jelly and change one letter (or the double letter) each time, building up a chain of linked words and making it end with jolly jelly or jelly jolly. There are lots of ways to do this, so it's a game that can be played often with different chains each time.

It can be played by one person or by two or more, as the players take it in turns to effect a change. Two people could play separately with a time limit so that they race to make as long a chain as they can in the time available.

A possible chain is this:

jolly	canny
jelly	catty
jetty	ratty
jerry	batty
berry	Betty
merry	belly
marry	jelly
carry	jolly

A 'j' word to syllabify: jew/el/ler/y – jewellery

This is a word that can also be spelt 'jewelry'. It appealed to me as a child and when I was doing a History topic on Roman jewellery at school I decided to use this more unusual spelling. My History teacher denounced it and insisted I correct it all the way through my topic, which – in the days before word processors – meant that my carefully written and illustrated topic was littered with corrections and ruined in my eyes! I can't bring myself to use 'jewelry' now, although it more closely reflects the way in which we pronounce the word as though it has just three syllables.

For 'jewellery', remember that a 'jeweller' makes 'jewellery' and that way your child will remember the third syllable. Ask your child if they know why we double the 'l'. Hopefully, if they have been paying attention, they'll roll their eyes heavenwards and remind you with infinite patience of the Harry Potter (doubling) rule!

A 'j' homophone: Jim/gym

Jim is a name that rhymes with Tim.

'Gym' is the short form of the word 'gymnasium' where we do 'gymnastics'.

The words are derived from the Greek language and many Greek words begin with 'gy'.

Your child may like to look up more words beginning with 'gy' as a reinforcement or extension exercise.

K is for Keith, K'Nex and Keyrings

Extra materials:

- Construction toy K'Nex
- Small pieces of card to laminate
- Keyrings (the type that clip open and shut)

Now, before you reach for the roll of wallpaper to draw round your child again and make a life-size model of Keith to add to your classroom characters, I should explain that I mention Keith here for a different reason.

In chapter I we covered the 'i before e' rule, but I did not mention that names with a long 'e' sound in the middle of the names are not governed by this rule.
The sharp-eyed among you may already have been wondering why Keith was not spelt 'Kieth' and that is why. Similarly, the names 'Sheila', 'Neil' and 'Deirdre' are spelt with 'ei'.

Silent k and K'Nex

One of the puzzles of the English language is why so many words include silent letters. Basically, the English language is a pot pourri of different languages – with influences from Greek, Latin, French, German, Anglo-Saxon and more.
The 'kn' beginning to a collection of words has a very interesting history. Although we do not sound the 'k' now, in the Middle Ages we did; thus, in Chaucer's introduction to his 'Canterbury Tales' he referred to a knight, which was pronounced 'k-nikt'.

SPELLING MADE MAGIC – An A-Z of spelling tips and tricks

The word 'knight' comes from the German word 'knicht', which is pronounced sounding the 'k' and which meant 'servant'. It was used especially for a servant of a knight , who would himself go on to become a knight. The Swedish sound the 'k' in their word for a knight, too – 'knekt'.

Many other languages, including Swedish, Danish, Norwegian and Dutch, all pronounce the 'k' in their 'kn' words. The word for 'knife' in Norwegian and Swedish is 'kniv' and their word for 'knee' is 'knä'. So you can see how spellings beginning 'kn' have been passed into the English language. It may help us to remember them if we actively sound the 'k' at the beginning of the words.

A well-known brand of stock cube did this as an advertising gimmick and promised their stock cubes would give chefs the 'k-now how'!

The word 'know' is derived from the German verb 'kennen', which is more recognisable in the Scottish version 'ken', as in "D'ye ken?"

Give your child the spelling 'know-how' by asking them to read these words sounding the 'k', then write them in unhyphenated form and pronounce them 'properly'.

k-nead	k-nee	k-neeler
k-neeling	k-new	k-nit
k-nitted	k-nitting	k-nob
k-nock	k-nocked	k-nocking
k-not	k-notted	k-notty
k-now	k-nowledge	k-nuckle

So, now you k-now!

SPELLING MADE MAGIC – An A-Z of spelling tips and tricks

A fun activity to reinforce this spelling might be to write a collection of 'Knock, knock' jokes and amuse one another at the tea table with them!

Another activity to help your child both associate the spelling with an activity and visualise the spellings would be to get the construction toy K'Nex out (or beg, borrow or buy some!) and fashion some 'kn' words out of the various pieces. Quite apart from the educational benefits, it is remarkably calming and therapeutic for you or your child to sit on the floor 'playing' with all those colourful plastic rods and connectors!

'K' homophones: knot/not and knight/night

One way to help your child distinguish between these homophones would be to explain the origin of the spellings, as outlined above. In addition, your child could emphasise the 'k' sound when saying the words 'k-not' and 'k-night', as opposed to the uncomplicated 'not' and 'night'.

Perhaps your child could write a funny story about a k-night and use as many 'k-n' words as possible to anchor the spellings in the memory.

A long 'k' word: knowledgeable

This would be a wonderful word to do a 'www exercise' with (see Chapter W) because this word contains so many small words. It easily divides into three recognisable words, know – ledge – able, which are easier to spell than the four syllables that make up the word. It would probably be easier for your child to remember the spelling by saying those three words aloud as they write them and then saying the completed word as it should be pronounced. Then you can praise them and tell them how 'knowledgeable' they are!

The 'k' rule:

'K' with an 'i', 'k' with an 'e'

Otherwise, always use a 'c'.

With two 'k' sounds to choose from, young children are often unsure as to whether to use 'curly c' or 'kicky k'. This rule helps them to decide, depending on the vowel that follows the 'k' sound.

cat	kitten
cot	ketchup
cut	

Read these words out to your child and see if they can work out whether the word begins with 'curly c' or 'kicky k', depending on the first vowel:

cotton	carry	kite	computer	Kent
cute	kitchen	kedgeree	cash	kilt
cord	keep	cushion	kiwi	captain
coral	curry	candyfloss	keg	cork
curl	kerb	curtain	copy	
cupboard	kettle	curtain	kept	kind

Remind your child that 'y' can act as a half vowel and sound like 'i', hence 'Kyle' and 'Kylie'.

The rule also works with 'sc' and 'sk',

scamp	skeleton
scooter	skill
scurry	sky

A good activity to help your child remember this rule is to get your child to call out 'k' and 'sk' words while skipping.

Keyrings

If your child has certain spellings to learn each week, you may like to laminate the words on pieces of card and attach them to the kind of key ring that clips open and shut. Your child can keep the key ring in their pocket and look at the words from time to time. The words can be changed each week and 'old' words kept in a small box and revised at regular intervals, so that they don't slip out of the memory. Once they have been well and truly passed into the long term memory, the pieces of card can be recycled.

'K' endings

In chapter J, we looked at the 'k' endings of words of one syllable, as in 'Jack' and 'Jake'.

If the short vowel is followed by a different consonant than a 'c', the word ends in a 'k'. Ask your child to think of some more examples for each column.

rk	nk	lk	sk
da**rk**	i**nk**	si**lk**	whi**sk**

SPELLING MADE MAGIC – An A-Z of spelling tips and tricks

If the word contains two vowels making one sound, the word ends in 'k'. Again, ask your child to add more examples to each column.

| **oak** | **eak** | **eek** | **ook** |
| cl**oak** | l**eak** | ch**eek** | c**ook** |

When a word has two syllables and ends in the 'ik' sound it is always spelt 'ic'.

Arctic   Atlantic   attic   fabric   music   mimic   panic   picnic

Can you think of any more?

L stands for laughter, lions and Lucky Luke!

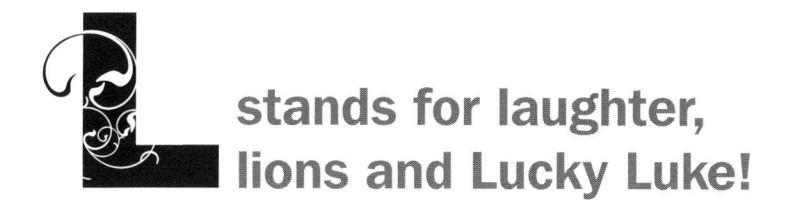

Extra materials needed:

Plastic bottles (small or large)

Laughter

I hope that you and your child have shared a few laughs while doing some of the activities in the last few chapters. It is so important to have fun while you learn and if you are relaxed, you are much more likely to learn than if you are feeling fraught or under pressure. The underlying aim of all my teaching is to make learning fun, so enjoy yourselves!

The word 'laugh' does not look at all as it sounds and therefore cannot be sounded out. It is one of those medium frequency words that need to be learnt in a different way. How about making up an acrostic and then drawing a picture of it? The spelling will be more memorable if you create the acrostic yourselves, but an example to get you started is:

Laugh At Ugly Gorillas Hopping

Lions

In long words, 'ion' is often found after a 't', making the 'tion' ('shun') sound, where the 'io' is not sounded as two vowels at all. A reading test I give pupils uses the word 'violinist' and it trips so many of them up. They are so used to vowel digraphs where the two vowels blend into a new sound, like 'oa', 'ei', 'au' and 'oi', that 'io' often takes young readers by surprise. Using the word 'lion' as an example, you can teach your child to divide the word into two syllables between the vowels: li/on.

The same rule applies to words with 'i' at the end of the first syllable and 'a' or 'e' at the beginning of the second. Ask your child to divide these words into syllables, between the 'i' and the second vowel and then read them correctly. Then you can change the order of the words and ask them to spell them.

| violin | diet | lioness | riot | Diana |
| giant | liar | biology | dial | quiet |

The 'le' ending

In chapters B and C I suggested different activities to spell the 'le' sound. As it is quite a tricky one, it is worth consolidating in different ways.

Another suggestion is to make an activity around the song 'Ten Green Bottles'. It is great fun to sing on journeys but why not make a wall display of cut out green bottles, each featuring an 'le' word and stuck on the display with blu-tac? Then play a game in which you take it in turns to remove a bottle, (at the end of each verse, if you are singing the song at the same time) and the other person has to guess which word has 'fallen down'! Keep on going until 'there are no green bottles hanging on the wall'!

Older children may prefer to take a real bottle and cover it in slips of paper, each featuring an 'le' word or to cut out bottle-shaped playing cards to make a Pairs game of 'le' words. The unusual shape of the cards will help them to visualise the spellings.

Lucky Luke

Another game to make, this time to reinforce the 'c' sound, spelt 'ck' or 'ke', is the card game 'Lucky Luke'. Basically, this is a variant on 'Happy Families', with Lucky Luke being the magic card which can complete any family of four.

The nine families are:

ack   eck   ick   ock   uck   ake   ike   oke   uke

You need to think of four words for each family. For example,

uck
duck
muck
luck
stuck

uke
duke
fluke
puke
rebuke

You may prefer to use 'jukebox' or another alternative for 'puke' but I'm sure your child will remember that card particularly! (Your child's history teacher will thank you for teaching your child the correct spelling of 'duke'. When I was teaching the Norman Conquest, William the Conqueror was referred to so often by my pupils in their writing as 'Duck William'. I am sure he would not have been amused!)

The easiest and most educational way to devise your families is to go through the alphabet, working out which letters can be combined with a particular ending, then choose the four you like best and write them each on a card. Repeat the exercise with the next ending and so on, until you have 36 cards. Your child may like to illustrate them with pictures cut out from magazines or drawn and coloured. You will also need two Lucky Luke cards that can be used to complete any family.

Shuffle and deal all the cards between the players. Any complete families or three family cards plus a Lucky Luke card can be placed down on the table. The youngest player then turns to the player on their left and chooses a card from their hand, with the cards carefully shielded so the chooser cannot see which card he is choosing. Thus, play continues around the players until someone wins by completing all their families. The winner must read their family words out correctly. If they make a mistake they must forfeit that family, so the ultimate winner is the player who completes the most families and reads them all correctly.

An 'l' homophone: lose / loose

The double 'o' is always followed by a soft 's' sound, as in 'moose' and 'noose'. 'Lose', like 'nose' and 'rose', sounds as though it contains a 'z'.

An 'l' word to syllabify: lo/ca/tion

Silent 'l' words

We met a silent 'l' word in chapter H in the word 'half'. Others combine with 'k', as in:

walk	folk
talk	yolk
stalk	
chalk	

Make some cards for a Pairs game from yolk-yellow card and decorate them with a border of a stalk with leaves growing from it. Association is a powerful memory tool. Your child will be able to picture the words on the distinctive cards and remember the spellings more easily.

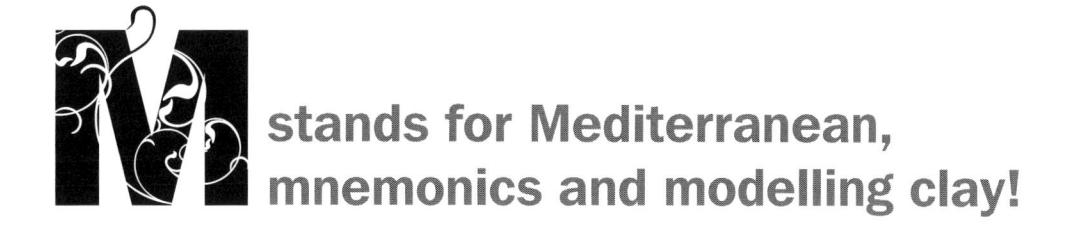

M stands for Mediterranean, mnemonics and modelling clay!

Extra materials needed:

- Modelling clay
- Camera to take a photo of your child with their modelling clay spelling model

I love the Mediterranean! Not just because the word conjures up blue seas, white sands and warm sunshine but because it is the most confidence-boosting spelling I have ever used.

Back in chapter C we built up that other lovely long 'm' word – mis/un/der/stand/ings. In my lessons I follow this spelling with 'Mediterranean', telling my pupils that they will be able to spell a word that many people find really difficult. Most people know that there is a double letter somewhere in the word, but is it double 'd', double 't', double 'r' or double 'n'? Chopping the words into chunks means that we use a double letter without even thinking about it!

Firstly, it is important to enunciate the word clearly. Many students spell it wrongly because they do not pronounce it correctly, saying 'mediterranium' as though it rhymes with 'geranium'. Then ask your child to count the number of syllables in the word, perhaps putting their hand under their chin to 'feel' the syllables as the jaw moves. You can then tell your child that after the first syllable of three letters, all the other syllables are just two letters long - easy peasy, lemon squeezy!

Most of the syllables are spelt phonetically, so spell just as they sound: med/it/er/ra/ne/an. The trickiest syllable is 'er' because there are so many ways to spell the 'er' sound, but as we found out in chapter E, 'er' gets the green light as it is the most common spelling. If you ask your child to spell 'med', then 'it', then 'er' and then 'ra', they will automatically spell the word with the double 'r'.

If they try to spell 'ra' as 'ray', praise them for remembering that a sunray would be spelt 'ray', but remind them that syllables are usually spelt as simply as possible, so 'ra' just needs two letters. I always pronounce the last syllable as 'an' to help them with the spelling, although, strictly speaking, the final syllable sounds as though it is 'un'.

Once you have spelt the whole word in this way, your child may like to write each syllable in a different colour or to alternate two colours to make the syllables stand out. They can photograph the spelling in their minds with their amazing mental camera and, when they feel ready, have a go at spelling it on their own.

I teach spelling to dyslexics at a College of Further and Higher Education and in my first lesson with students I ask them if they could spell a 17-letter long word. They usually look aghast, but proceed to spell 'misunderstandings' perfectly, as I build up the word in the same way that we did in chapter C. When I tell them we are going to spell a word most people find difficult but they will find easy, they look at me as though I am crackers. But I guide them through the syllables and they spell 'Mediterranean' perfectly. By now my students are looking quite chuffed with themselves so I give them a challenge. I ask them to go and ask their classmates if they can spell 'Mediterranean'.

One girl who accepted the challenge had told me she was 'rubbish' at spelling and scored herself 4 out of 10 for spelling. When I saw her the next week, she was walking tall and quite delighted with herself. No-one in her class had been able to spell 'Mediterranean' and she was now the class' 'spelling guru' and her class mates came to her for spellings. Her confidence soared and she taught them the principle of chopping words into chunks.

Mnemonics are memory aids and come in all shapes and sizes. You can memorise dates, facts, general knowledge and more. Countless school children have learnt the colours of the rainbow with the mnemonic 'Richard of York Gave Battle In Vain' but did you know that 'Rowntrees of York Give Best in Value'?

The points of a compass going clockwise round are remembered with the mnemonic 'Never Eat Shredded Wheat'! The order of the planets going outwards from the sun is remembered with the phrase 'My Very Easy Method Just Speeds Up Naming Planets'.

The acrostics and plays on words (like 'I to the end will be your friend') that we have mentioned in this book so far are all forms of mnemonics. You can put facts and spellings to music or rhythm if you like, as we did with the 'd' rule in chapter D and as we will do in chapter W with the worst word in the English language…!

A tricky 'm' word: many

My mnemonic for this word, which looks as though it should be pronounced 'man-y' and sounds as though it should be spelt 'menny' is 'Many a man likes football!' The point of the mnemonic is to help them see the connection between 'man' and 'many'. Once they can spell 'many', they can knock off the 'm' and spell 'any'. So you get two spellings for the price of one!

SPELLING MADE MAGIC – An A-Z of spelling tips and tricks

An 'm' word to syllabify: mul/tip/lic/a/tion

Because we do not always enunciate words clearly, many children hear the word as 'multipication' and omit the 'l'. Remind your child that it comes from the mathematical process 'to multiply', where the 'l' can be clearly heard.

A memory game: My aunt went to market…

You can make up any number of variations on this, but the general principle is that you work through the alphabet and each player must recount the previous items before adding their own. This is a wonderful game to play on a journey or at a family gathering, as well as in a lesson; it develops memory strategies and encourages more descriptive vocabulary, as well as testing your child's knowledge of the alphabet. Young children might find it challenging enough to remember one item for each letter, whereas older children will probably enjoy adding descriptive words.

As an example, you might say "My aunt went to market and bought some (appetising) apples". The next person would repeat what you had said and add, "and some (badly bruised) bananas." A third player (or the first player if there are only two of you) would recall, "My aunt went to market and bought some appetising apples, some badly bruised bananas and … some crimson cherries." Thus the game continues. You may not have time to get to the end of the alphabet but you could always stagger the game over two or three days, which will further test your memories!

This game is particularly effective in a large group. The tendency is to associate the item with the person who chose it, so you look round the group at each person to jog your memory. The game can be used as a party game or introductory activity where everyone describes themselves with an adjective beginning with the same letter as their Christian name and must remember everyone else's name and adjective before adding their own to the list.

Alternatives are:

I went to the zoo and saw …. (animals)

For Christmas I got … (increasingly outlandish presents!)

If I could go back in history I would like to have been/met … (historical figures)

If I had a private jet, I would fly to … (countries and/or cities of the world)

Months of the Year

Some of the spellings of the months are quite difficult, especially if they are mispronounced in the first place. 'February' often catches youngsters out, as they mishear it as 'Febuary'. Remind them that it is a winter month and when they go out into the cold, they probably say "Brrr!" so they must put the 'br' in February.

Similarly, some children think the first month is 'Janury' and omit the 'a'. The chant for the months of the year is quite helpful as it enunciates the syllables, Jan/u/ar/y, Feb/ru/ar/y, March …

Often the chant is enough to teach children the order of the months but some get confused by the order of the 'ber' months, September to December. I like to show them the name made by the first letter of the last six months:

January	**J**uly
February	**A**ugust
March	**S**eptember
April	**O**ctober
May	**N**ovember
June	**D**ecember

The name spelt out is Jason D. Children familiar with Jason Donovan may like to think of him.

You could incorporate a little history lesson and teach the children the Roman numbers that lend themselves to some of the months. In the Roman calendar, which began with March, September was the seventh month, October the eighth month, November the ninth and December the tenth. Your child will be familiar with other 'oct words, such as the 'octopus' with eight legs and an 'octagon' with eight sides. The 'decimal' system is based on the number 10 and the word 'decimate' comes from the killing of one soldier out of every 10 when a battle was lost.

Your child may like to research the other names of the months as a history project and it will introduce them to Roman gods, goddesses and emperors.

'M' homophones:

meat / meet   The easiest way to distinguish between these two words is to think 'You **eat** m**eat**'.

If it helps to have a phrase for 'meet', you could think 'You m**ee**t friends you want to s**ee** again.'

Or perhaps you can think of a better one!

made / maid   Differentiate between these by thinking, 'The maid does the ironing!'

Modelling clay

In 'the Gift of Dyslexia' by Ronald D. Davis,[1] which turns around the widely held notion that dyslexia is a disability, Davis explains why dyslexic readers have difficulty decoding little words, such as 'with', 'by' and 'that', but can read longer words with no trouble. Dyslexics usually think in pictures and associate words with specific pictures, as we mentioned in chapter I, so they see a picture of a dog, when they read the word 'dog', but get no picture to associate with the word 'do'. Davis suggests getting the modelling clay out, not as a diversion or a remedy for frustration, but to create pictures to go with those words which have no natural picture. First, think of an interesting sentence that includes your target word and then bring the sentence to life in modelling clay. Next, spell the word out in modelling clay letters. Finally, take a picture of your child with their spelling model. The photograph is then stuck in a 'Spelling Magic' book headed by the tricky word in big letters with the sentence underneath the photograph.

In this way, your child can build up a special vocabulary book, which they can look through and use to gradually memorise the words by visualising the picture and associating the picture with its particular word. In the photograph below,

Georgina has brought the word 'for' to life with reference to her favourite treat – chocolate brownies!

1. Davis, Ronald D. (1995) The Gift of Dyslexia .London: Souvenir Press

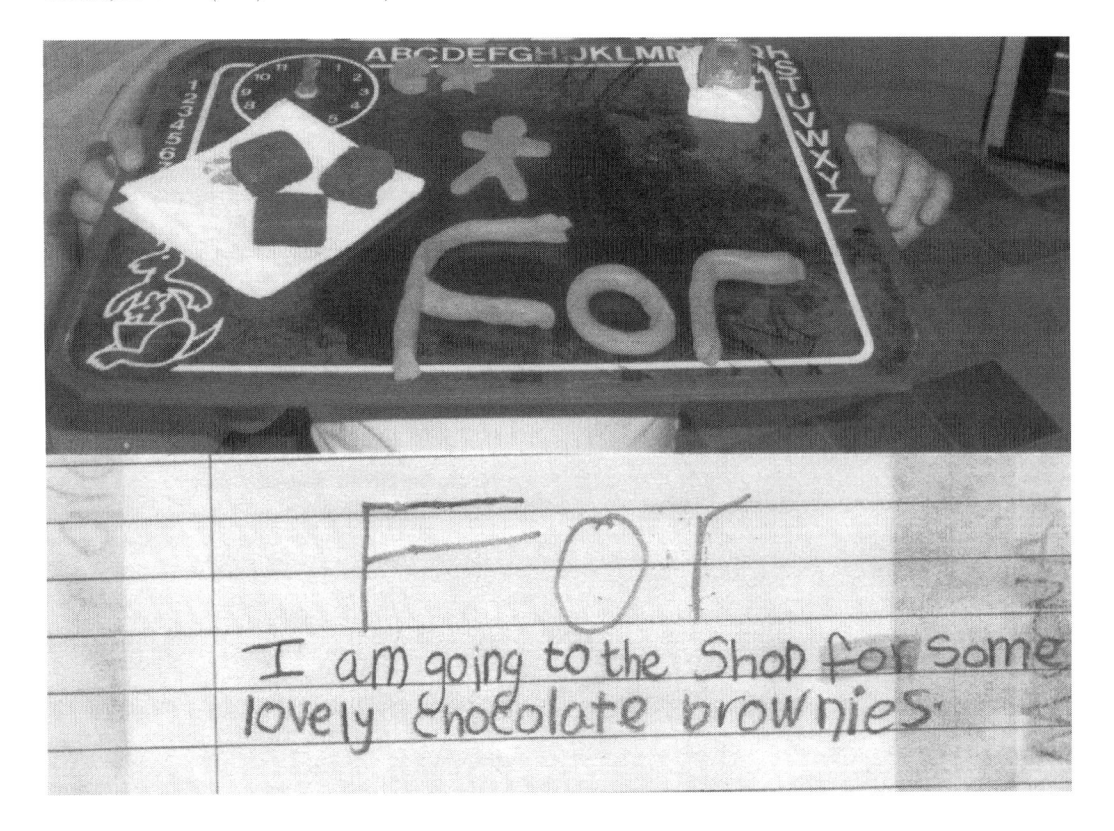

N is for names, numbers and the Lone Ranger

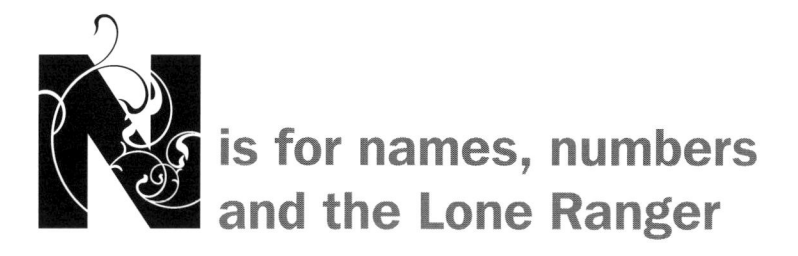

Extra materials needed:

- Old photograph negatives
- Matchsticks
- Rubber gloves
- Small pale-coloured candle (or use stumps of old birthday cake candles)
- Washing-up sponge
- Ink

Names

It is worth capitalising on names and making displays around your child's name or surname. Your child can write and decorate their name as attractively as possible and put it at the hub of a display, with words that rhyme with it shooting out from it. So, as mentioned in Chapter D, Paul could inspire a host of 'au' words, Sue – a collection of 'ue' words, Josh – 'sh' words and so on.

The name 'Stephen' once inspired an unusual display from my students in which the letters for various 'ph' words were cut out of unwanted photographs. This helped the youngsters to visualise the spellings and associate the 'ph' sound with photographs. We also edged the display with strips of negatives, to compound the association. It is helpful to use different media for your displays to make them more memorable – and this is a great way to use up all those negatives and extra photographs you can't bring yourself to throw away!

Surnames often provide similar opportunities for creative vocabulary extension. Brown helps with the 'ow' sound, Jones with the silent 'e' and Smith with the 'th' sound. So think about your family names and see what spelling magic you can create with them.

Numbers

While your child may be fluent in counting their numbers, they may be less confident about spelling them.

One: Even the first number is tricky to spell, as it sounds as though it would be spelt 'w-o-n', but , of course, it is actually spelt 'one'. The magic 'e' does not make the first vowel long, but you could say that it changes the 'o' to say 'wo'!

Enter the Lone Ranger – one ranger on his own! If your child is comfortable with spelling 'lone', which does conform to the magic 'e' rule, then teach your child the connection between 'lone' and 'one'. When they are happy with spelling 'one', it would be a good idea to throw in the spelling of 'once' as well, so that your child can see and hear the similarity between the two words. They may like to write their own fairy story beginning 'Once upon a time' and see how many times they can use the words 'one' and 'once' in the story.

A more pictorial approach to the word is to attach an acrostic to the word 'one' and illustrate it. So your child might like to draw a picture of nine chubby owls, surrounding a rather skinny owl, with the caption 'One owl never eats!' You could, of course, substitute octopuses or any other creature beginning with 'o' for the owls, or devise a completely different acrostic. The more thought you put into an acrostic or picture, the more likely you are to remember it later.

Two: The easiest way to remember the unsounded 'tw' at the beginning of the word 'two' is to think of 'two twins'. Other words connected with 'two' also sound the 'tw' – 'twelve', 'twenty' and 'twice'.

Your child may like to stencil, write or print out each word six times and stick the words on playing cards. You now have 30 cards that you can play Snap with, using two piles of cards so you can easily see when the word is duplicated on the other pile. You could also play Pairs with them. If you write each word in a different font or colour, it becomes more of a challenge to spot the same word.

Three: Young children who are learning the 'ee' sound may like to play a version of Fizz Buzz. Take it in turns with your child to count from 1 to 36. Obviously, you will say 'three' at the right time, but from then on when you reach a multiple of 3, say a word that rhymes with 'three', instead of saying the number! Possibilities include 'me', 'sea', 'aunty' and so on.

If you want to reinforce the double 'e' spelling, you could say any word that contains 'ee', such as 'meet' or 'bee-hive'. It helps to count in threes on your fingers, so you know when to substitute an 'ee' word.

Older children who can cope with the triple consonant cluster 'thr' could say words beginning with 'thr'. If the adults playing can think of longer or more unusual 'thr' words, you will help your child to broaden their vocabulary.

Four: This is one of three homophones – for, fore and four. Help your child to see that the number 'four' has four letters in it and a 'u' to indicate it is a number.

Five: How about creating a spelling sparkler for the number 'five' with other 'ive' words emanating from the number five at the centre?

Six: Make a hexagonal spinner (with six sides) and divide it into six segments. A matchstick through a hexagonal piece of card about 5cm wide should suffice. In one segment write 'ax', in the next write 'ex', then in the following segments write 'ix', 'ox' and 'ux'. In the last segment, in smaller letters write 'inx' and 'ynx'. Take it in turns to spin the spinner and when the spinner lands on an ending, think of a word with that ending and write it down. Words can only be used once and the winner is the first person to write down a pre-determined number of words.

Seven: This is quite a straightforward spelling, although it could stimulate a brainstorming session with your child of words that end in 'en', such as 'garden' and 'kitchen'. They may be tempted to spell 'heaven' the same way as 'seven'; remind them that there are angels in heaven!

You could also make a pairs game of five very similar words with different pronunciations:

seven   even   sever   ever   every

Eight: This is one of those awkward 'ght' words we dealt with in chapter G. It is probably worth combining 'eight' with 'height' and 'weight' and throwing in 'eighteen' and 'eighty' for good measure! Can your child think of a sentence or a limerick using all five words?

Your child may like to draw a picture evoked by the following acrostic: '8 elephants in green hats totter' or one of their own devising. Or as a family, have a competition and see who can compose the best acrostic for 'eight'.

An 'n' acrostic: necessary

This is one of my favourite acrostics ever! I call it the secret of eternal youth!

Never **E**at **C**hips, **E**at **S**almon **S**andwiches **A**nd **R**emain **Y**oung.

One of my students told me this mouth-watering version:

Never **E**at **C**hips, **E**at **S**almon **S**andwiches **A**nd **R**aspberry **Y**ogurt.

The main problem with the word is that people are never sure if there is one 's' and two 'c's or one 'c' and two 's's. Your child could think of a shirt that has one collar and two sleeves to help them remember.

An 'n' homophone: no /know

When I was young, I was often told firmly, "N – o spells 'no'." If your child confuses 'no' with 'know' perhaps that would help. In chapter D we tackled a group of two letter words ending in 'o', so hopefully your child is very familiar with 'no' by this time.

As we mentioned in chapter K, it can be helpful to sound the 'k' sound at the beginning of 'silent k' words, to give them the 'k-now how'!

Silent 'n' words

In Chapter A we mentioned that the silent 'n' at the end of 'autumn' can be remembered by thinking of the adjective 'autumnal', where the 'n' can be clearly heard. Other words that end in a silent 'n' can also be extended in such a way that we can hear the 'n'.

The silent 'n' in 'condemn' can be heard in 'condemnation' in the same way that the silent 'n' in 'damn' can be heard in 'damnation'.

A 'hymn' is found in a 'hymnal', a 'columnist' writes a 'column' and from 'solemnity' we get 'solemn'.

You and your child can play 'Match ups' if you write each of those words onto cards and place them face down on the table. Match up the silent 'n' words with their corresponding spoken 'n' words, in the same way that you would play Pairs. Do test your child on the spelling of the silent 'n' words to ensure they are remembering to include the silent 'n'.

An 'n' word to syllabify: nom/in/a/tion

Inky fingers!

The 'nk' sound is quite hard to hear, so an enjoyable activity to reinforce this sound entails the use of a candle and some ink or poster paint. It is advisable to cover your table with newspaper, give your child rubber or plastic gloves to wear, to avoid the afore-mentioned inky fingers, and supervise the activity very carefully – especially if ink is used.

Brainstorm with your child as many 'nk' words as you can. It is helpful to work through the alphabet consistently with first 'ank', then 'ink', 'onk' and 'unk'. Several initial consonant blends combine with various endings, including 'th', 'bl', 'cl' and 'shr'. You can also add suffixes as appropriate, such as 'donkey', 'monkey', 'conker', 'hanky' and so on.

Fold a sheet of A4 paper into 18 rectangles, by folding the long side into three columns and the short side into six. Now take a small, pale coloured candle (or wax crayon); this is a good activity for using up stumps of birthday cake candles. Your child can write one of your 'nk' words with the candle into one of the rectangles. It will be almost invisible!

Continue until all the rectangles have an 'nk' word in them. Then paint over the whole sheet of paper with a strong colour or dip a piece of washing up sponge in some ink and spread it over the paper. The 'invisible' candle writing will now magically be revealed by the paint or the ink!

Once dry, the paper can be cut into the rectangles and your child can mount them on cards to use in a card game of your choice. You could play Happy Families, collecting sets of four 'ank', 'ink', 'onk' and 'unk' words, or duplicate some of your words and play Pairs or Snap.

O is for onions and double 'oo's'!

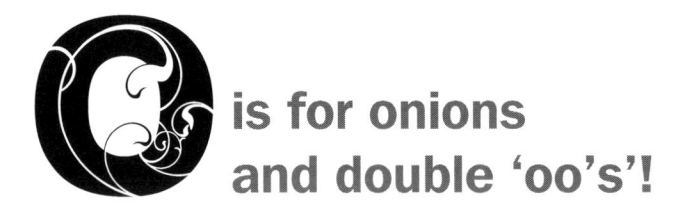

Extra materials needed:

Bananas, cherry tomatoes, grapes and/or potato hoops

Can you work out what this word is?

Is this any clearer?

The word is written in joined italic writing. If it was written in a rounded style it would look like this: uniun

In italics, the 'u, 'n' and 'i' letters are so similar that they cannot be told apart. This is why the 'u' was changed to 'o', so that words could be decoded more easily, and 'uniun' became 'onion'!

Know your onions!

Change the 'u' in these words to 'o' to see how to spell them correctly:

duve	luve
uther	shuve
nuthing	bruther
gluve	guvern
muther	abuve
pulice	cuver
anuther	guvernment

An 'o' acrostic

This acrostic can be used with three awkward words – could, would and should.

The root of all three words is 'ould' or 'Old Uncles Lie Down'.

Could = **C**ould **O**ld **U**ncles **L**ie **D**own?

Would = **W**ould **O**ld **U**ncles **L**ie **D**own?

Should = **Sh**ould **O**ld **U**ncles **L**ie **D**own?

Another way of remembering the spelling of the 'ould' is to think of the phrase "O u lonely duck."

An 'o' rule: To make words ending in 'o' plural, add 's' or 'es'.

For musical words ending in 'o' just add an 's'. So,

piano	–	pianos	solo	–	solos
alto	–	altos	soprano	–	sopranos
banjo	–	banjos	disco	–	discos

A common 'o' word, 'photo', also just takes 's' – 'photos'.

Words that take 'es' in the plural can be remembered in pairs:

Potatoes and tomatoes (edibles)

Tornadoes and volcanoes (natural disasters)

Cargoes and torpedoes (carried on a ship)

Echoes and heroes (two syllables)

Mosquitoes and dominoes (three syllables)

An 'o' homophone: of /off

Often children spell 'of' as 'ov', which is an understandable error. At least they know the word comprises just two letters, so perhaps they can simply substitute an 'f' for the 'v'.

Perhaps the simplest way to differentiate the two words is to combine 'off' with another 'ff' word. For example, you could encourage your child to think, "Fred fell off the cliff." To emphasise the 'f' sound we double the 'f' in 'off'.

An 'o' word to syllabify: o/ver/pow/er/ing

And, finally, to those double 'oo's'!

When teaching your child the 'oo' sound, whether short as in 'look' or long as in 'moon', try using slices of banana, cherry tomatoes, grapes cut in half, or potato hoops. When you child has made up lots of 'oo' words around them, they can eat the edible 'o's' and write in their place the double 'o'.

The power of association as a learning tool helps to firmly etch this activity into their memory, as they picture the fruit making the 'oo' sound and as they associate the pleasurable experience of eating the 'oo' words they make.

You could revisit coding vowels with your child and, as you think of an 'oo' word, code it with a smile for the short 'oo' sound or with a line for the long 'oo' sound. Can you see any patterns? Which words take the short 'oo' sound?

Another way of consolidating the 'oo' sound in your child's phonic bank is to use a magic screen that has a noughts and crosses stamp. Your child can write the words on the screen and stamp the double 'o' with the nought stamp. Novelty is a very effective way of reinforcing a new sound and your child will remember the activity more easily.

Having mentioned the word 'look' as an example of a short 'oo' sound, here is a visual aid to remember the spelling; it also differentiates it from 'luck'. Just as we 'see' with two eyes, so we 'look' with two eyes, so ask your child to make the double 'o' into eyes.

look see

P is for plurals, pies and pea shooters!

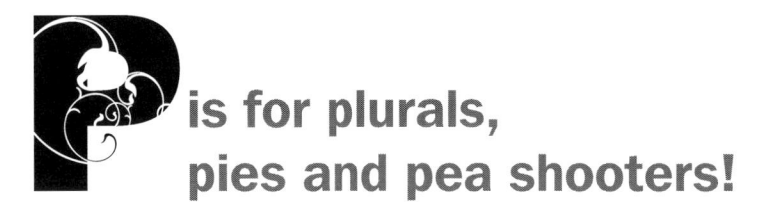

Extra materials needed:

You don't need any extra materials for this chapter.

Plurals

In the last chapter we made plurals of 'o' words. In some cases we had to add 'es' not just an 's'. We sometimes have to add 'es' to make other words plural, if they end in what we call 'sibilant' sounds. These are letters that are sounded like a hiss – s, x, z, ch, tch, and sh.

If you think about it, it is very difficult to make 'box' become 'boxs' without it becoming a second syllable and, as your child knows, every syllable should have a vowel, so we add the 'e' as well as the 's'. If you add an 's' to the word 'glass', you would have a ridiculous number of 's's and it would still sound as though you had added a second syllable. So we write it as 'glasses'.

Some verbs (doing words) also need 'es' added, instead of just the 's', after sibilant sounds. For example, a bee 'buzzes', a snake 'hisses' and Dad 'fixes' the washing machine. Often these verbs double up as nouns, but the 'es' ending applies to both.

Take a piece of A4 paper and lay it down horizontally. Fold it in half lengthways and then fold it into three lengthways so you end up with six columns. Put one of the sibilant sounds at the top of each column and brainstorm with your child as many words as you can that end with those sounds. Your child can write them in the column and add the plural version. Which column has the most words?

You may already have made a Pairs game for the 'o' plurals from the last chapter, so if you like, you can add some more to the game or make a new set of Pairs to match up the singular to the plural form.

Plurals of words ending in 'y'

In Chapter C, we came across the rule 'Change the 'y' to an 'i' when you add an ending'. This also applies to plurals of words that end in 'y' and we add 'es'. So, 'pony' becomes 'ponies' in the plural and 'lady' becomes 'ladies'. Can your child put the following words into their plural form?

berry	cherry
poppy	lolly
mummy	daddy
granny	aunty
penny	copy
jelly	curry

In Chapter V we shall look at plurals of words that use 'v', in Chapter Y tackle plurals of words ending in 'y' and in Chapter Z look in more detail at plurals of words ending in 'z'. There are some words that are the same whether they are singular or plural; they include two animals – deer and sheep and two fish – trout and salmon.

Some words are always found in their plural form. They can often be referred to as 'a pair of ...'. Such words are:

SPELLING MADE MAGIC – An A-Z of spelling tips and tricks

trousers and braces   shorts and pants

scissors   straighteners and tongs

I was recently asked why we talk about a pair of pants. I guessed it was to do with the fact that there are two leg holes in a pair of pants just as trousers and shorts have two 'legs'. Scissors, straighteners and tongs both have two parts.

Two other words are always found in the plural – measles and suds – probably because you never come down with just one measle and it would be difficult to produce just one soap sud!

Unusual plurals

Of course, the English language has to have some words that do their own thing completely! So the plural of 'man' is 'men' and the plural of 'woman' is 'women' (although it is usually pronounced as though it is 'wimmin'!)

Three 'oo' words change to 'ee' in the plural:

Tooth – teeth   foot – feet   goose – geese

(but mongoose becomes mongooses!)

Finally, the plural of 'mouse' is, of course, 'mice'!

Pairs

From being a young child I can remember playing Pairs games with my family and I always seemed to win! I don't know if that's because they let me win or because our memories get worse as we get older, so children have the advantage over their elders.

Now that I play Pairs with my pupils, I think the latter is the correct explanation because the youngsters remember cards they picked up several turns ago, whereas I forget them very quickly. Whatever the reason, Pairs is a great game to play with children to help them develop memory strategies and to boost their confidence when they keep beating you hands down!

By now, you may well have quite a collection of Pairs games and the danger is that if they are all on white card they may blur into one game. It can be helpful to encourage your child's powers of association by using different colours, shapes and media for each game. This is why, for instance, I suggested you use your Easter egg boxes to cut up into irregularly shaped flash cards – or into regular cards for Pairs games.

Cornflakes boxes can be cut up into a pack of cards to feature 'or' words or 'magic e' words. Cereal packets and other food boxes are ideal to cut up into packs of cards ready for when you want to make a new game. Just the colour of the cards will come to be associated with those particular spellings. In the past, I have used blue card for 'wa' spellings, because of the association with water, and orangey-gold coloured card for 'au' words, because Au is the chemical symbol for gold and autumn is the time when the leaves turn gold.

Some 'p' homophones: passed / past, piece / peace

The 'ed' at the end of 'passed' tells us that it is a verb in the past tense. 'Past' is not a verb so must not be used in place of a verb. This sentence may be worth learning and writing out a few times to help differentiate between the two:

In the race, Ed passed Rob, then ran past Chris to win.

'A piece of pie' is a well-known mnemonic for this homophone.

I have heard several variations on the pea-shooter theme, but 'Pea-shooters give us no peace' is as good a mnemonic as any.

Your child may also have come across a 'peace treaty' in their history lessons, both words featuring the 'ea' blend.

A 'p' homograph: present

Where a homophone has the same sound but different spelling, a homograph has the same spelling but different pronunciation and different meaning. In the two versions of 'present', the emphasis changes from the first 'e' to the second.

'Pres**e**nt', with the emphasis on the second 'e', is a doing word or a verb.

A 'pr**e**sent', with the emphasis on the first 'e', is a noun. If you are not sure whether to spell the second syllable with an 'a', an 'e' or a 'u', think of the phrase, "I present you with a present."

Mind your 'p's and 'q's!

If your child struggles to remember the orientation of these letters, the trick that we learnt in Chapter B to remember the shape of 'b' and 'd' can be utilised.

Once again, your child should give you the thumbs up with both hands, giving you the 'b' shape with the left hand and the 'd' shape with the right hand. If they then twist their wrists so that the thumbs point downwards, the left hand forms the letter 'p' and the right hand forms the letter 'q'.

A 'p' word to syllabify: pal/in/dromes

Pal in what?!! A 'palindrome' is a word or sentence that spells the same backwards as well as forwards. Simple examples are 'pip', 'pop' and 'pup'. The names 'Eve', 'Anna' and 'Hannah' are also examples.

What does the following sentence say if you read it backwards, rearranging the spaces to make the words intelligible?

"Was it a cat I saw?"

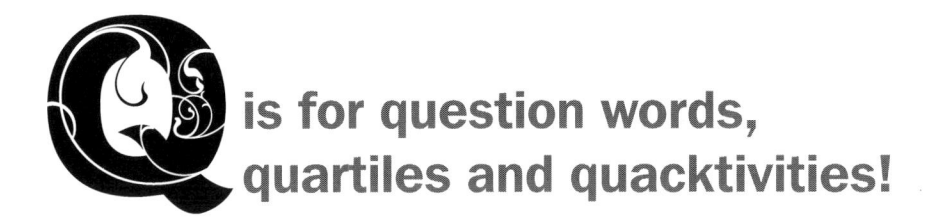

Q is for question words, quartiles and quacktivities!

Extra materials needed:

You don't need any extra materials for this chapter.

Question words

Most of the question words begin with 'wh':

Who   where   when   what   why   and   which

The exception is how.

To help your child remember these words, draw a large two-dimensional question mark on a poster-sized piece of coloured paper or card. Then ask your child to stencil or print out the words in bold lettering and stick them on the question mark. The word 'how' should be stuck on the 'dot' under the question mark. Display the poster where your child will see it and learn to remember the words.

The order of the words is helpful when your child has to write a story. I used to encourage my primary school pupils to plan their stories by thinking;

Who were the characters in the story?
Where did it take place?
When did the story take place?
What happened in the story?

If your child has to write a review of a story, they can add

Why they liked or disliked the story?

For tips on spelling these words, look in Chapter W.

Question word bingo

Make a spelling die, as shown in Chapter D. On each face of the die write a 'wh' question word. Print out grids of nine spaces (three by three) and, at the start of the game, each player writes a 'wh' question word in each space. (Some words will obviously be used more than once.)

Players shake the spelling die in turn and put a counter or button on their grid, depending on which word is thrown. You can see who gets a horizontal line first, then who gets two lines and, finally, who wins with a full house. It's addictive stuff!

A 'q' rule

In the English language, wherever the letter 'q' is found, it will always be followed by the letter 'u'.

When spelling the word 'cucumber', some children intelligently try to spell it 'qcumber'. If your child is tempted to do so, remind them that every syllable should have a vowel and encourage them to listen to the consonant and vowel that make up the first syllable, c-u-cumber.

Quick 'qu' activity (quack-tivity?)

Divide two A4 sheets of paper into four columns and in the columns put headings qua, que, qui, and quo. Then set a timer for five minutes and see how many 'qu'

SPELLING MADE MAGIC – An A-Z of spelling tips and tricks

words you and your child independently can think of to write in each column. At the end of the time limit, you can exchange your results and see who got the most.

You can be generous to your child and leave the common 'qu' words for them to write down, but you could extend their vocabulary by writing down such words as 'querulous', 'quizzical' and so on in your columns.

Once you have brainstormed all the 'qu' words you can both think of, you could tackle an extension exercise where you look in a dictionary for other 'qu' words. Your child is bound to learn several new words to include in their vocabulary and they may like to start a little vocabulary book, perhaps in an alphabetised book such as an address book, in which they write new words and their definitions.

A 'q' homophone: quite / quiet

Strictly speaking this isn't a homophone as the words do not sound identical, but their similarity leads to confusion. 'Quite' has just one syllable whereas 'qui/et' has two.

Give your child two cards, one featuring the number '1' and the other with number '2'. Rapidly fire the words 'quiet' and 'quite' at your child and they must respond by holding up the card with the correct number of syllables.

An alternative activity would be to draw a picture of ET, as was suggested in Chapter E, with the caption "ET is quiet."

To consolidate the 'ite' ending, your child could draw a spelling sparkler with 'quite' in the centre and other 'ite' words sparking out from it.

A tricky 'q' word: queue

This is a lovely word to spell once you put the letter names to a rhythm –

Q,u e,u e.

Someone once said that a queue always doubles, which is why we double the 'u' and 'e'.

In French, the word 'queue', pronounced 'cuh', means tail. A queue does look rather like a tail, doesn't it?

Quartiles

These are related to quarters and refer to the division of a dictionary into four sections, to facilitate finding one's way around it. The first quartile obviously begins with 'A'. Not so long ago, if you took a dictionary and opened it at the half way point, you would 'land' in the 'M' section. If you divided the first part of the dictionary in half again, you would probably open it at the 'E' section, the second quartile, while the second half would be divided and reveal the 'S' section, the fourth quartile.

A mnemonic was devised to help children remember the quartiles, thus:

All Elephants Make Squirts!

If a child wanted to look up a word beginning with 't', knowing that 't' followed 's' in the alphabet, they would divide their dictionary into quartiles and look for the word in the third quartile, just after the 's' section. Similarly, if they were looking up a word beginning with 'g', they would turn to the second quartile.

Nowadays, so many new words have been added to the dictionary that the quartiles fall at different places, usually A, D L & R

Your child may like to devise their own mnemonic for the quartiles in your dictionary. A young pupil of mine remembers them in this way:

All Dead Lions Regenerate!

R is for raps, Rudolph and rice paper!

Extra materials needed:

- Old Christmas cards
- English coins
- A computer and access to the internet
- Rice paper
- Icing pens or tubes

Roots

Now, before you think you are reading a gardening book, I shall hasten to reassure you that the roots of which I am thinking are parts of words! Over half the words in the dictionary have Latin roots; that is to say that the main part or stem of the word comes from the Latin. To these roots we add beginnings and endings, or prefixes and suffixes.

If we take the word 'recycling', the root word is 'cycle'. The prefix, put in front of the root, is 're', which means 'again' or 'afresh'. At the end of the root word is the suffix 'ing'.

Sometimes it helps us to spell awkward words if we think of their root word. For example, the root 'multiply' helps us to remember to include the 'l' in 'multiplication'. At other times, it can be helpful to think of extended words in order to spell a tricky root word. The root word 'sign' is not pronounced as it looks, so cannot be sounded out. If we think of a long word with the root 'sign' – 'signature', this will help us hear the letters s-i-g-n.

Another tricky word is 'similar'. Bearing in mind that we have said that the most common way of spelling the 'r' suffix is 'er', your child would be forgiven for spelling it as 'similer'. If you think of the extended word 'similarity', you can hear the 'a' and can correctly spell the suffix 'ar'.

Raps and rhythm

It is worth investing in some of the wonderful books of raps around now, because raps have made poetry 'cool' to a generation of youngsters. In my experience, youngsters delight in watching adults trying to rap. They will love to clap or click their fingers to the beat. It's always a hilarious treat for children to see their parents or teachers attempt to rap!

Children love the regular beat of raps and encouraging them to read raps themselves will give their reading the support of a steady rhythm and boost their confidence in reading aloud. It will foster a love of words and appreciation of rhyme that will bear dividends when they are trying to spell.

'Rhythm' is a really difficult word to spell. Your child may like to make up an acrostic to help. Otherwise, they could remember that;

Rhythm **h**elps **y**ou **t**o **h**um **m**usically.

Another 'r' acrostic: right

Ride **I**n **G**ranny's **H**elicopter **T**onight

And then you'll get the spelling right!

I know we mentioned this acrostic in Chapter G, in connection with those tricky 'ght' words, but a little repetition helps consolidate a difficult spelling.

Some 'r' homophones: right /write, read /reed and rain /rein/reign.

Right/write

The most helpful way I can offer to differentiate these two is to say, "You write with a pen." That should remind your child to begin the word with a 'w' and then the rest of the word is a straightforward magic 'e' word.

Right can be remembered with the above acrostic, which puts the word into an appropriate context.

I'm aware that there is a third homophone – 'rite'. For young children, it is probably enough to cope with right and write, without confusing them with a third. For older children who are familiar with the word 'rite', you could tell them that the word is linked to 'ritual' but that to change the 'rit' in 'ritual' to 'rite', they need to add the magic 'e'.

Read/reed

I'm not sure how often children need to be able to spell the word 'reed' but the best way to differentiate between the two homophones is to think, "You read a book," and picture green reeds.

If your child would like a visual prompt to help them remember 'reed', they could draw a picture of an animal, such as a seal, otter, hippo or crocodile, swimming in water, surrounded by reeds and bullrushes. If they draw the animal with just the curve of their head and their eyes visible above the water, they could make the two eyes into two letter 'e's and write the 'r' and the 'd' on either side of the face and draw long green reeds around it. Or they could simply draw the picture and write the word 'reed' underneath in green with two eyes for the 'e's.

Rain, rein, reign

Rain obviously has to be colour-coded blue! One easy way to help with the spelling is to draw a raindrop over the 'i' instead of a dot.

To remember the 'e' in 'rein', your child could colour or download a picture of Father Christmas holding the reins of his reindeer. Or you could devise another acrostic for your collection. I like the picture of Rudolph the Red-Nosed Reindeer evoked by this acrostic:

Rudolph **e**njoys **I**talian **n**oodles

I can just see him sucking up the noodles like spaghetti! If you want to extend your child's vocabulary, you could substitute 'ingesting' for 'Italian' and think of another word with the root 'gest' that we use more often than 'ingest'.

Your child can then add this acrostic to the collection in their acrostic book and draw a picture of Rudolph eating noodles or, if you have any old Christmas cards around, they could find a card featuring Rudolph and stick this under the word 'rein'.

I have colour coded 'reign' with royal purple. This is one of those gnome words we discussed in Chapter G, where the 'g' is silent. Although the word comes from the French word, 'reignier' – to reign, your child may be familiar with some Latin based words to do with royalty, which contain the 'g' sound. An example is the word 'regal' which means 'royal'. Show your child the back of an English coin and ask them to find the word 'reg'. Can they guess what it means?

The Latin inscription round the coin says that Elizabeth II is Queen by the grace of God. The word 'reg' is short for 'regina' which means 'queen'. Perhaps this information will help your child remember the 'g' in 'reign'.

A fun activity to reinforce this is to take part in some coin rubbing. Your child could use wax crayons to take rubbings of different coins or make lots of rubbings in different colours of the same coin – front and back. Having cut out all the coins, position them on a large piece of paper to spell the word 'reign', with each letter made up of a chain of coins!

A shorter or complementary activity could be to write the word 'reign' in big letters and make the circle of the 'g' into a face, draw a crown above it and make the curved down stroke into an arm, holding the orb that is given to newly crowned kings and queens. If you want to include a little history lesson, encourage your child to look on the internet for some pictures of Queen Elizabeth I. There is a beautiful portrait of her wearing fabulous, bejewelled clothes and holding a golden orb in her left hand.

An 'r' word to syllabify: reg/u/lar/ly

Can your child remember that other long 'r' word we chopped into chunks in Chapter I – re/spon/si/bi/li/ty? Can they also remember how to put it into the plural and which rule to apply?

Rice paper spelling

It's a while since we did any edible spelling, so how about buying some rice paper and icing pens and letting your child write some spellings on rice paper? They could decorate some buns or biscuits with rice paper words or write their spellings of the week on rectangles of rice paper and eat them once they have spelt the words correctly in a later test! Bon appetit!

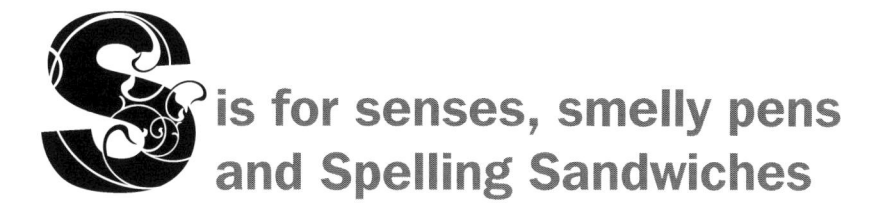

S is for senses, smelly pens and Spelling Sandwiches

Extra materials needed:

- Dice

- Blindfold

- A piece of "hidden treasure" (a toy or edible treat)

- Sandpit, sand and plastic or wooden spade (or head to the beach for some outdoor spelling!)

Senses

Despite the crazy title, I have not taken leave of my senses! When working with dyslexic youngsters, it is important to harness as many senses as possible to facilitate learning, and what is good for dyslexics is good for all. As well as adding a new dimension to learning, multi-sensory learning encourages accelerated learning while having fun.

This is one of the reasons I continually advocate edible spelling, so that the sense of taste is included in the learning experience and the accelerated learning tool of association is employed. The sense of smell is not used very often in traditional learning, although my revision strategies for older students include the use of a range of fragrant sprays!

This is where smelly pens come into their own! Commercially available in sweet 'flavours' or smells, these pens can revolutionise writing and spelling. If your child is struggling with a certain blend or consonant cluster, ask them to choose a particular smelly pen and write as many words as they can with that blend or sound, inhaling the smell as they spell! When they need to remember those words for a spelling test for instance, they should smell that pen again and the association of the smell with the spelling should make the words rush back into their memory.

At other times, use different smelly pens and different sheets of paper for other spelling exercises. See whether your child can remember which pen they used with which spellings and ask them whether they remember the spellings more easily when they smell that pen again. It may just seem a gimmick, but if it works with a difficult exercise, whether because of its novelty value or not, it will encourage your child. At the very least, they will associate the activity with a bit of fun, which will help them to develop a positive view of spelling.

Spelling Sandwiches

In my experience, children are attracted by anything to do with food! Learning spellings can sound a lot less attractive! 'Spelling Sandwiches' combine the two. In school, children are often taught to use the 'Look, cover, write and check' method of learning to spell, which uses two senses – the visual sense and the kinesthetic (motor) sense.

The 'Simultaneous Oral Spelling' method (SOS) adds two more senses – the aural (hearing) and the oral (speaking). This is where the child says and, therefore, hears the letter names or sounds as they write them. Spelling Sandwiches combine the 'Look, cover, write and check' method with SOS.

- After looking at the word to be spelt and covering it, the child says the word aloud. (The bread)
- The child then says the letter names or sounds as they write them. (The filling)
- The child says the word again to anchor the letter names or sounds to that word.

(The top slice of bread)

• They can then check that they are correct.

It is important to say the word that has been spelt after sounding out or naming the letters, so that one does not think 'f-r-o-m' spells 'frog'. If your child is still at the stage of sounding out letter sounds, they should continue to do that in their Spelling Sandwiches. If they are competent at naming the letters, they should do the same with their Spelling Sandwiches. Either way, I would suggest they have just three or four words to practise each night, preferably the irregular sight words like 'right', 'their' and 'could' that cannot be spelt phonetically and need to be learnt.

An 's' rule: The 'soft c' rule

In Chapter K we covered the 'k' rule with a rhyme. This rhyme continues to explain the soft 'c' rule:

'K' with an 'i', 'k' with an 'e',

Otherwise, always use a 'c'

Because 'c' with an 'i' and 'c' with an 'e'

Go soft, you see.

Words that contain 'ci' or 'ce' sound as though they use the 's' sound. A good example of both is 'city centre'. Your child will probably be quite familiar with words that end in 'ce', including 'space', 'dance' and the over-used 'nice'! They may be less confident with words beginning with 'ce' and 'ci'. Just changing one letter can make all the difference to a word. For example, changing one letter makes 'curtain' become 'certain.'

Give your child two cards to hold, one displaying the letter H for 'hard' and one with S for 'soft'. Ask them to listen to these words and then decide whether the first sound is hard or soft and hold up the appropriate card.

kitty	city	country	circle	cut
ketchup	curtsey	celebrate	custard	central
cider	cattle	cave	kitchen	celery
cuddly	cereal	certificate	curtain	curry

Now, divide a piece of paper into three columns. At the top of one, write 'Hard', at the top of the next column write 'Soft c + e' and at the top of the last write 'Soft c + i'.

Then read the words aloud again and see if your child can decide in which column the word should be written and encourage them to write the words themselves in the correct column. You can talk them through any difficulties so that they learn from the activity.

In spelling, stumbling blocks can always be converted into stepping stones!

Space race

You may like to incorporate some astronomy into your lesson by making this game! On some white paper, draw a ribbon divided roughly into blocks. Then your child can paint or colour a space scene in the background, with different planets, stars and constellations.

Next, divide a piece of paper into three columns, headed 'ace', 'ice', 'uce' and brainstorm as many words as you can for each column. Then write the 'uce' words at intervals in the band and fill the remaining spaces with an equal number from your 'ace' and 'ice' columns.

Your child can make some rocket counters out of card to fit the spaces (i.e. 4cm by 2cm) and then you can get ready for the 'Space Race'. The object is not to race to the end of the game, but to be the first player to collect a pre-determined number of each type of word, with no duplications!

Each player has a piece of paper with three columns, headed 'ace', 'ice' and 'uce' and a pen. The first player throws a die, moves the appropriate number of spaces, reads the word they have landed on and writes it in the correct column on their playing sheet. Play continues, moving round and round the board until the winner is declared.

Adding 'ed' and 'ing' to words ending in 'c'

Now that your child understands that 'c' with an 'i' goes soft, they will understand why we have to add a letter after a word ending in 'c' to stop the 'ed' or the 'ing' changing the 'cuh' sound to a 'suh' sound. As in the Harry Potter doubling rule, we double the consonant, but instead of using 'cc', we use 'ck'.

Thus, 'panic' becomes 'panicked' and 'panicking' and 'picnic' becomes 'picnicked' and 'picnicking'.

An 's' acrostic: said

Your child may like 'Save Animals In Distress' or may prefer to make up an acrostic of their own, perhaps starting with the word 'said' as a prompt.

'S' homophones: see /sea, seen /scene and sight /site

In Chapter O, we tackled the spelling of two 'visual' words, 'look' and 'see' by drawing eyes in the double letters. If your child draws eyes in 'see' and 'seen' it will help them to differentiate those words from their homophones.

You see with your eyes. The 'sea' with an 'a' has waves.

You have seen with your eyes. There was a scary scene in the script.

Sight/site: We have come across a few 'ight' words now and after the work you did in Chapter G, your child should be more confident about spelling the 'ght' words.

Why not construct a spelling sparkler around the word 'sight' to refresh your child's memory for the 'ight' words or write some sentences using 'sight' and other 'ight' words. For example: the sight of the ghost last night gave me a fright!

With the popularity of the internet and the commonplace use of the word 'website', your child may be quite familiar with the idea of 'site' being a place. If not, you could have a treasure hunt with them, at the end of which you instruct them to "Sit on the site of the treasure!"

Blind Man's Treasure Hunt

In a pair, one player is blindfolded and the other hides a piece of treasure – a toy or piece of fruit for example – on the floor or on a chair somewhere in the room. The second player must give instructions to the blindfolded player that leads them to the treasure. When they are in position the final instruction can be, "Sit on the site of the treasure."

A tricky 's' word: soldier

This sounds a very blunt way of remembering the 'i' in 'soldier, but if you remind your child that, "A soldier is prepared to die for his country," they can see the word 'die' in 'soldier'.

An 's' game: Syllable Snap

This is a lovely game for your child to make and an interesting variant on the many Pairs games you will have made by now! Your child should look through a mail order or shop catalogue or some magazines and cut out small pictures to mount individually on playing cards. For each picture you will need the number of syllables in its name on a card of a different colour. So you will end up with a pack of picture cards in one colour and a pack of number cards in a different colour.

To play Snap, you take one pack and your child has the other. Both piles should be well shuffled. Take it in turns to put a card down on the table, making one pile. When a card is put down with the same number of syllables as were in the previous or following picture card, the first person to shout 'Snap' adds the pile of cards on the table to their pack and play resumes until one person is holding all the cards.

To play Pairs, spread out all the picture cards, face down, on one half of the table and place the number cards face down on the other half. Take it in turns to turn over one of the picture cards and then try to find the matching number of syllables in the word from the number cards. You may have to lay down some rules as to whether a little bit of licence is allowed for either Snap or Pairs – for example, if you turn over a picture of a football, can you accept a 1 card for 'ball' as well as a 2 card for 'foot/ball'?

The game can lead to some interesting discussions about syllabification, such as whether 'camera' is two syllables or three. The word is pronounced 'cam/ra' with two syllables, however strictly speaking the word has three syllables! The idea of the game is to enjoy it and practice syllabification skills, not to fall out over it!

Sandpit spelling

In Chapter G, we mentioned using sand trays or salt trays in which to practise writing letters or spelling words. A sandpit, of course, is just a bigger version but with the added excitement of taking a spelling lesson outdoors! If you want to go the whole hog, you can go off to the beach for the day and write in the sand to your heart's content! An added bonus of this is that you can do some wonderful calligraphy in the sand, using a child's spade to effect 'thick and thin' lettering.

Stepping stones

This is a very popular activity with both girls and boys and simply involves tearing some sheets of A4 paper in half and writing on each one a letter from the spellings of the week. Thus, if your child is learning some magic 'e' spellings, you could write the following in big letters on your stepping stones – i, l, m, k, s, p, n, b, h and e.

Spread the stepping stones out on the floor and ask your child to spell a word by stepping from one letter to the next in the correct order. If they prefer they can hop or jump from letter to letter and you can move the letters around and further apart to vary the challenge. It is a great way for children to expend surplus energy, to revive them if they are getting a little tired or to inject even more fun into your lesson!

T is for teddies, trains and trigraphs

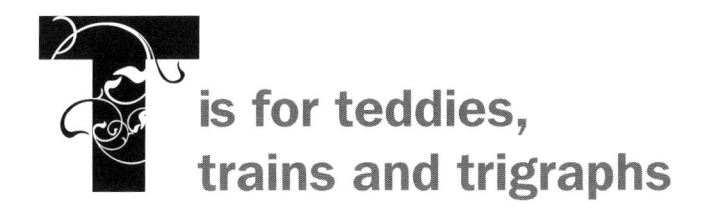

Extra materials needed:

Scrabble letters

Ted words

The only two things I could ever draw at school were teddy bears and daffodils! The teddies finally came in useful when I wanted to help young spellers spell the 'ed' ending when it tended to sound like 'id', often at the end of a verb ending in 't'.

- Draw a large teddy on a piece of paper or in your child's exercise book and brainstorm with your child lots of verbs ending in 't', so that you can put them into the past tense and create 'ted' words. Some verbs, like 'create', end in 'te' and so you simply add a 'd' to put it into the past tense, but you still make a 'ted' word.
- Simple verbs to start you off are: start, want, count, grate, and nest. You could also refer to your life-size classroom friend, Ed, that we created in Chapter E.
- Two-syllabled words include: direct, arrest, relate, and connect.
  To challenge your child and/or extend their vocabulary there are some impressive polysyllabic words they could convert into 'ted' words, including: aggravate, inundate, co-ordinate.
- A tricky 'ted' word: benefited
  Because 'fitted' doubles the 't' to stop magic 'e' from making the first vowel go long, it is tempting to double the 't' in 'benefited' also. However, because the stress is not on the 'i' we do not need to double the 't'.

Ben and fit Ed benefited from lots of exercise.

A 't' rule

If a word ends in 'till', drop the second 'l'. e.g. until, distil.

Two 't' acrostics: thought and through

These are tricky words because they share so many of the same letters. Encourage your child to hear the 't' sound at the end of 'thought' and the 'r' sound at the beginning of 'through'. These acrostics may help, especially if your child brings them alive by illustrating them and sticking them in their acrostic book.

Tom **H**as **O**ne **U**mbrella, **G**ary **H**as **T**wo.
Ten **H**airy **R**ound **O**ranges **U**se **G**reen **H**air **S**pray!

Some 't' homophones: their/there/they're, to/too/two, toe/tow

Our work in Chapter C on contractions may have helped your child to remember the 'they're' that is the contraction of 'they are'. Similarly, in Chapter H we tackled the here/hear homophone with reference to the triangle of 'Words of Place', in which all the words contain 'here'. So the word 'there' that is to do with place or fact (for example, there are hundreds of stars in the sky) contains the word 'here'.

The homophone which seems to cause the most trouble is 'their'. It is to do with belonging, so if it can be followed by a noun, such as 'their cat' or 'their dog', 'their' is the correct version to use. I teach my pupils to think of the phrase,

Their eyes are blue

because it contains the 'i' sound and the 'r' sound in the correct order after the letters 'the' which begin each of the homophones.

To/too and two

To has a short sound and so is the shortest word of the three. The word too that sounds like the number two, but from the context is clearly not the number two, has two 'o's. Say some sentences containing the words to and too and ask your child to tell you if the word is short or long. This will help them distinguish one from the other and help them spell the words correctly.

As we mentioned in Chapter N with the numbers, two is easy to remember if you think of the related words twins, twice, twelve & twenty.

Toe and tow

Your to**e**s are on your f**ee**t.

You to**w** a boat through **w**ater.

Tricky word tracking

It is quite helpful to devise a 'tracking' exercise to help your child spell short, tricky words like 'their'. The idea is that you write or type a stream of random letters and incorporate the letters in order from 'their' several times. Your child then underlines the letters until they come to the first letter of 'their', a 't', which they circle, and then underline the letters until they can circle an 'h', then an 'e', an 'i' and a 'r'. The example below, is for the word 'goes'.

goes   hkgluonbeputszcgljoqprejhsbdcbolmbeaitwsgd

The train game

If your child is finding 'their' tricky to spell, write the letters that make up the word twice over on little squares of paper. Alternatively, your child could find two sets of the correct letters from a Scrabble game and turn them over, face down, on your table. The idea of the game is that you take it in turns to turn over a letter, aiming to find a 't' first, then an 'h' and so on. There should be enough letters for each player to be able to build up the word, but the first player to manage it is the winner. It's a very simple but effective way of memorising a tricky spelling in a game format.

A polysyllabic 't' word: tem/per/a/ture

It is quite easy to see the individual words 'rat' and 'temper' in this big word. Under the title 'Temperature' your child may like to draw a picture of a very red-faced rat looking very annoyed, with the caption, 'U r a rat in a temper!'

Tests and tables

If your child is having difficulty learning tables, especially if they are dyslexic, break the table down into manageable chunks, as we do with the spelling or reading of long words. Thus, they should learn just the first four lines of the table, saying each line aloud as they write it, so that they employ a multi-sensory approach, as we did with spellings in Chapter S.

Once they are confident with those four lines (after a week, say) move on to the next four. Ask them to say the first four lines aloud, before writing the next four, so that they consolidate their knowledge of the first four lines, while adding the next four. After another week or a few days, they can say aloud the first eight lines, then begin writing the last four lines, still saying them aloud.

Many of us parents will probably remember the dreaded weekly spelling test, often of completely random, unconnected words, that we had to prepare for when we were at school. Sadly, this is still the practice of some schools and it can be a nightmare for dyslexic youngsters or those who find spelling difficult. I encourage teachers to allow children to choose how many spellings they can realistically learn that week and then aim to reach that target.

If they can spell easily, children will usually opt for 10 out of 10, but it takes the pressure off those with learning difficulties if they can look at the words for the test and decide how many they can cope with. They are unlikely to be lazy, but are likely to set a manageable target for themselves. Then they should feel a justifiable sense of achievement when they meet that target, rather than a sense of frustration and failure if they have tried to learn all 10 words and only managed to spell three or four.

Trigraph words

These are consonant clusters of three letters – hence 'tri' graphs. They include chr, thr, shr, str, scr at the beginning of words and 'dge' and 'tch' at the end of words.

It is worth noting that although there are two initial consonant clusters with the same sound, 'sc' and 'sk', there is only one corresponding triple cluster – scr.

The 'tch' trigraph is used after single syllable words with a short vowel, with the exception of these words:

rich, which, such, and much,

which are worth learning as a separate group.

SPELLING MADE MAGIC – An A-Z of spelling tips and tricks

A patchwork quilt

This lovely activity involves some mathematical work in creating some tessellating hexagons out of different coloured pieces of paper and sticking them onto some display paper . You and your child could brainstorm as many 'tch' words as you can and type, write or stencil them out and stick them on to the hexagons. Alternatively, if you are Harry Potter fans, you may like to stencil these words out and stick them in order on the "quilt" as a memory aid to 'tch' words:

Watch the witch catch the snitch on the Quidditch pitch.

U is for fruit juice, biscuits and Bob the Builder!

Extra materials needed:

Computer keyboard

A 'u' rule:

The long 'u' sound is made in several ways and I find it helpful to put four of them into window panes where you can see the similarities between them. They are less common than the 'oo' sound heard in 'moon', which can be drawn like a pair of eyes above a 'u' nose, representing words like 'usual'.

oo

u

ue ui

eu ew

Encourage your child to look for the similarities between the vowel digraphs and think of examples of words for each one. It is good to select a key word or two for each one that you can write across each corner of the window and 'fruit juice' is a good example for the 'ui' sound.

With the euro a common currency now, you might choose 'euro' or 'Europe' as your key word for 'eu' or if your child is studying the feudal system in history, they may prefer 'feud'.

The 'ue' sound also includes 'u-e' so you could choose a word with each spelling for your keywords.

As always, the English language throws in some unusual words, like 'do', 'shoe', 'view' and 'through', which can be written underneath the window, once your child is familiar with the four digraphs in the window panes.

Young spellers and the long 'u' sound

Young spellers may need to spend time on individual digraphs, perhaps revising u-e first, then moving on to 'ue' words. At a later date teach your child the 'ew' spelling, perhaps to coincide with New Year and later still the 'eu' sound, so that they do not confuse all the spellings if taught at the same time.

Older spellers, who are familiar and confident with these long 'u' digraphs, can progress to the more unusual 'ui' vowel digraph. Words containing 'ui' should ideally be learnt and practised on the keyboard, where the letters 'u' and 'i' are next to each other, so your child can use the correct fingering for touch typing with those letters at least. Thus, they should type 'u' with the pointer finger of their right hand and the 'i' with the taller, middle finger. Get them to practise 'ui' with those two fingers over and over again, before adding 'ui' words.

Typing tricky spellings to a rhythm is a good idea; you can type 'fruit' to the rhythm   f - r- u i - t

                                             1 - 2 - 3 and - 4

'Juice' can be spelt to the rhythm   j- u - i c - e

                                             1 - 2 - 3 and - 4

Alternatively, or in addition, you could sound the words as they are spelt, to help your child 'hear' the 'u' and 'i' sounds within the words. Thus, 'fruit' looks as though it should be pronounced 'froo-it', while 'juice' looks as though it should be pronounced 'joo-ice'.

Older spellers may enjoy memorising the window of long 'u' digraphs, with the face above it, and compiling lists of words for each sound. Every day, you could give them a blank window to complete with the digraphs and key words.

Play 'Give us a Clue' together, where one of you thinks of a long 'u' word and gives the other clues as to what the word is so that they can guess what it is. A point is awarded if they can spell the guessed word correctly. The winner of the game is the player with the most points!

Silent 'u' words

Bob the Builder introduces us to an exception to the 'ui' sound, where it makes a short 'i' sound instead of a long 'u' sound, because the 'u' is silent. It comes from an Old English word and, although 'build' and words stemming from it (builder, building etc) are the only examples of words beginning with 'bui' in the dictionary, its frequency in the English language may explain why so many young spellers want to spell 'business' with the 'bui' beginning.

Another common exception is the word 'biscuit', which literally means 'twice cooked' and comes from the Latin 'bis coctus' and the French 'bis cuit'.

The silent 'u' is frequently paired with 'g' to keep the 'g' hard in words where the following 'e' or 'i' would soften the 'g'.

guess	guest	guide	guilty	guitar
guy	disguise	guillotine		

Your child could write, type or stencil all these 'gue' and 'gui' words out and stick them onto playing cards, then practice dictionary skills by putting all the words into alphabetical order.

Play 'Guess the guy'. From the pack of cards, choose one. Your partner must write down which card they think you have, until they guess the correct one. Then swap over. The winner of the game is the player who guesses the correct word in the least number of (correctly spelt!) guesses.

A 'u' homophone: you /ewe

These are two other ways of spelling the long 'u' phoneme and these, of course, are words in themselves. 'You' sounds as though it should be spelt 'yu' but if your child finds it difficult to remember the 'o' in the middle, ask them to draw a smiley face in the 'o' to make the word more attractive and memorable.

The 'ewe' for a female sheep, with its two curly 'e's, always makes me think of the curly horns that some sheep have. It also has two 'e's just as the word 'sheep' does.

A 'u' mnemonic

The 'ur' sound often trips up young spellers, who are more used to seeing the 'er' version of the phoneme. Here is a clever way to remember the 'ur' in the word 'church'.

The following billboard is put outside a church to encourage people to come in.

Ch   ch

What's missing?

You are!

The 'un' prefix

This simply means the opposite of the word that follows it. So;

Unlike = not like

Undone = not done

Unkind = not kind

Unhelpful = not helpful

What does unnecessary mean?

A long 'u' word: un/u/su/al/ly – another word to stick on Al and Ally!

V is for vowels, elves and television

Extra materials needed:

- Rubber gloves
- Felt or other fabric, googly eyes, wool etc for making finger puppets

Vowels

When your child is learning the vowels a e i o u, it can be fun to give him or her a rubber glove to wear with a vowel written on the front and back of each of the five fingers! Then you can say a vowel sound and your child can wiggle the appropriate finger.

You can progress to saying cvc words (short words consisting of a consonant, a short vowel and another consonant, like 'cat') and your child has to listen out for the vowel and flex the appropriate finger again. A variation on this is to make finger puppets for each vowel, perhaps featuring an image to associate with it, such as an apple for the 'a' and an umbrella for the 'u'.

In Chapter C we looked at coding long and short vowels. If your child is quite confident with the vowel sounds, you might like to give them two rubber gloves or two sets of finger puppets, one hand for the short vowels and one hand for the long vowels. Once again, you can say a word with a long or short vowel and your child must work out whether the vowel is long or short and flex the appropriate finger.

Teach your child that every syllable must have a vowel. When they come to spell polysyllabic words, some words sound as though they have no vowel in the first syllable – words like 'decide' and 'behave'. As long as your child remembers that every syllable must have a vowel, they will have a better chance of spelling such words correctly.

There is a little rhyme that says,

When two vowels go out walking
The first one does the talking.

It means that when two vowels are seen together only the first vowel is pronounced and it is usually the name of the vowel that is said. It is not true for every vowel digraph but it will help your child to read the following: ai ea oa ee ie ei oe ue ui.

A 'v' rule:

No English word ends in a 'v' (except for the old-fashioned slang word 'spiv'). It will always be rounded off with an 'e'. e.g. love, five, save.

Plurals

When words ending in 'f' become plural, the 'f' changes to a 'v' and you add 'es'. Thus, 'elf' becomes 'elves'. Put these words into the plural:

wife	loaf	thief
life	half	wolf
knife	calf	shelf
leaf	shea	

147

A 'v' homophone: veil/vale

A vale is the same as a valley; you can hear the 'a' in 'valley' so keep the 'a' in 'vale' also.

The other veil is worn at a wedding and covers the eyes, so it includes an 'e' and an 'i'.

A polysyllabic 'v' word: vis/u/al/i/sa/tion

At first glance this is a difficult word to spell, but if you listen carefully to the component sounds and chop it up into syllables, it is more manageable. Note that the two 's' letters are pronounced as a 'z'. Your child is probably familiar with the 'z' sound spelt as an 's' in the word 'television', so you may like to talk your child through the various words that stem from 'vision' and 'visual', which all use a 's' for the 'z' sound.

vision	visual
revision	visually
television	visualise
visualisation	

You now have two more words to add to Al and Ally, if you have not used them already.

Visualisation

This is a powerful accelerated learning tool and is a skill worth teaching your child, as it will pay dividends in later years when they have to remember their revision notes for exams. It doesn't have to be a chore, just encouraged in gentle, everyday ways. For example, ask them if they can picture in their minds the birthday cake they had last year or their first teddy bear. Every now and then, ask them to remember something visual, such as the view from the hotel they stayed in or who they sat with at a birthday party.

We all have a preferred learning style:

Visual – we learn best by looking at books, watching DVDs, by colour coding notes and/or 'photographing' them.

Auditory – we learn best by hearing a teacher talk about a subject, listening to tapes, especially of our own voices reading out notes to learn, putting spellings or key dates to music and changing the words of popular songs to information that needs to be learnt and so on.

Kinesthetic – we learn best by doing, through practical activities. This is why young children learn through play and why it is important to back up new concepts and teaching with lots of practical examples.

Ideally, teaching should encompass all three styles, which is why multi-sensory teaching is good for everyone. Your child may not necessarily be a visual learner, but with the popularity of television from an early age, children are used to information being presented visually and respond to it.

Dyslexics, in particular, think in pictures, as I explained in Chapter I. Words conjure up pictures in their minds and they associate the picture with the word. The little words that proliferate in the English language, like 'the', 'of', 'with' and 'from', have no picture associated with them, so we have to create our own as described in Chapter M. It is worth making a visual dictionary for the words your child struggles with and going through it with them regularly, asking your child what sentence and picture they created for a certain word. This will encourage their ability to visualise and help with their spelling. Two for the price of one!

W stands for witches and Walt the Wizard

Extra materials needed:

Blank postcards

A 'w' rule: Walt the Wizard changes vowels!

- Walt the Wizard changes 'a' to the short 'o' sound

  because the short 'o' sound after a 'w' is spelt with an 'a':

  was, watch, what.

- Walt the wizard changes 'ar' to 'or'

  because the 'or' sound after a 'w' is spelt 'ar':

  war, warm, warn.

- Walt the wizard changes 'or' to 'er'

  because the 'er' sound after 'w' is spelt 'or':

  worm, world, worst.

From the picture you can see how your child could make a display showing Walt the Wizard's magic. The 'wo' sound is also heard in words like 'swan', 'quarrel' and 'squash'.

Walt the wizard changes vowels.

If you make a different display of 'war' words, you could cut letters out of newspapers to form the words. There are often references to war in the papers so your child could cut out all the 'war' words, particularly if they are in bigger type in headlines, and add other letters to them to make 'war' words, such as 'warm' and 'ward'.

'W' homophones: wear /where/were, which /witch

For 'where' we once again refer to the Words of Place triangle, in which all the words contain the word 'here'. It is also a question word and if you made the poster in Chapter Q, you will remember that all the words in the question mark begin with the letters 'wh'.

For 'wear', think "You wear earrings."

'Were' is not necessarily a homophone; it depends how you pronounce it, but children tend to confuse it with 'where' when they are writing.

Encourage your child to feel the shape of their mouth as they enunciate 'where' with a big, wide mouth and note the difference when they say 'were' with a more scrunched up mouth! Being aware of the different sounds is half the battle.

Another tactic is to point out the 'we we rule'. Pardon? The what?
If you think about it, we never say "We where……." But we do say "We were….." 'Were' is a verb and therefore always follows a pronoun – 'you', 'we', 'they' etc. If you can teach your child the 'we we rule', they will hopefully remember to use it to help them decide whether the word they are looking for is 'where' or 'were'.

Ask your child to write out 'where' and 'were' in two different colours on two postcards, one word on each. Then have a bit of fun together, taking it in turns to be teacher who says "where, were, were, were, where, were, were, where" and so on, while the 'pupil' has to hold up the correct card. You can go faster and faster until the cards are a blur and the muscles in your mouth are aching!

Then the 'teacher' can think of sentences using 'where' or 'were' and say them aloud for the 'pupil' to hold up the correct card again.

A 'w' acrostic: witch

Witches In Their Crooked Hats

This helps with that other common homophone: which/witch. Once again, you can refer to your question mark poster to point out the 'which' you would use at the beginning of a question, which begins with 'wh'.

A tricky 'w' word: walk

So many children understandably want to spell this 'wark' but, of course, Walt the

Wizard has worked his magic on the letters. Encourage your child to see the 'legs' in the 'l' and the 'k' and perhaps draw little feet on them to associate the letters with the action of walking.

Alternatively, pronounce the word as it looks, to rhyme with 'talc'. At least that way, your child can hear the silent 'l' in 'walk'. Or, tackle it in a group of 'lk' words, like talk, stalk and chalk, making a spelling sparkler of it. (See Chapter B.)

Another enjoyable and tactile activity with any group of tricky words is to take it in turns to write one of the words on each other's backs with a finger. It really focuses the mind on the 'feel' of the letters and the novelty of the exercise will help those particular spellings to be remembered.

A 'w' polysyllabic word: Wed/nes/day

This is one of those words that is easier to spell when sounded out as the word is written or as it has been divided into syllables above.

And, finally, the worst word to spell in the English language…

(in my opinion) …is

who

I know it's only three letters long, but it doesn't sound anything like it looks and doesn't look anything like it sounds! It looks as though it should be pronounced 'wuh-ho(t)' or 'wuh-hoe'.

Who sounds as though it should be spelt 'hoo'. I can understand why so many children think it is spelt 'h-o-w', because you can hear the 'h' at the beginning and a 'w' at the end and so their visual memory reminds them of 'how' and they insert an 'o' in the middle. Right? No, unfortunately. Wrong.

Dr Who to the rescue! Visual learners may well remember the spelling if they see the name 'Dr Who' regularly but there is another fun way of remembering the spelling using the Dr Who theme tune. Drum the rhythm of the theme tune while singing or saying the letter names in time to the rhythm:

w-h, w-h, w-h, o, w-h, w-h, w-h, o, who!

X is for Xmas, xylophones and exercise

Extra materials needed:

- Marzipan
- Ready-to-roll icing
- Toy xylophone

Personally, I take exception to the way that some people spell Christmas as Xmas! I wonder if it is because the 'chr' trigraph confuses them. Christmas, of course, means 'the birth of Christ' and of the Greek letters that spell Christ, the 'c' sound is made by the Greek letter 'ch'.

If you ask people what they associate with Christmas, among their answers will probably be carols, holly and robins or cake, holidays and Rudolph. Ask your child which three things they would like to associate with Christmas that begin with 'c', 'h' and 'r' and that will help them remember the beginning of Christmas and other 'chr' words as well.

As I have mentioned, my theory of spelling xtra-long words originally featured a Christmas cake, as it would be a daunting challenge to eat a whole, rich, fruity Christmas cake in one go. Reading and spelling long words can be similarly daunting and this is why we chop the words into chunks or syllables. Many of the children with whom I have worked wrinkled up their noses at the mention of Christmas cake and as you will appreciate by now, I am concerned to foster positive associations with spelling, not negative ones. For this reason, I changed the cake in the theory to a massive chocolate gateau.

When you are icing your family Christmas cake, do save any leftover pieces of marzipan and ready to roll icing, as they are ideal to use for a little edible spelling! Your child will enjoy making letters to spell their words of the week, then once they have learnt the spellings, they can eat their words!

An 'x' rule: for nouns that end in 'x' add 'es' when they go into the plural

As we said in Chapter P in connection with plurals, it is very hard to say 'boxs' without adding a second syllable. Because every syllable should have a vowel, we add the 'e' as well as an 's'.

Ask your child to put these nouns into the plural:

box	fox
fix	flex
tax	cox
sex	six
hex	mix
jinx	reflex

An 'x' homophone: except /accept

There is a clear difference between these words if the initial vowel is articulated carefully. However, they come from the same root 'cept', from the Latin for 'take'.

When 'ex' is added to a word it means 'out' (think of an exit, which is a way out) so 'except' literally means 'take out' (but not the American form of a takeaway!)

Remember the difference in meaning by thinking, "You accept a gift."

In the English language, words never begin 'axc'. The sound is always made with a double 'c', a hard 'c' first and then a 'c' softened by the following magic 'e'.

Conversely, in the English language only one word begins 'ecce' – the word 'eccentric', which can actually be spelt 'excentric' and literally means 'ex centre' or 'out of the centre'. The sound is usually made with 'exc'.

Exercise

From the way we say this word, it sounds as though it should be spelt 'excercise', but it comes from the verb 'to exert', which gave us the noun 'exercise', which has since become a verb in its own right.

A polysyllabic 'x' word: ex/tra/or/din/a/ry

It is worth chopping this word up into syllables so that one hears the first 'a' in 'extra'; so often the word is pronounced 'extrordinary' as though there is no 'a'.

Xtraordinary people

The British Dyslexia Association has long championed the cause of dyslexics and has set up a web site for these extraordinary people.

Dyslexics are an amazingly talented bunch and if you know dyslexic youngsters who may be struggling at school, encourage them with the fact that Einstein was a dyslexic and that their brain is wired up the same way as his!

Dyslexics have special talents, as though to compensate for their specific learning difficulties. They make outstanding designers and architects because of their superior spatial awareness and their ability to look at a two dimensional map or plan and see it in 3D.

They excel at practical jobs and because they have to devise their own coping strategies become adept at problem solving and seeing possibilities where others fail to do so. This often makes them entrepreneurs and also, in many cases, millionaires! So, dyslexia is not a disability; it can be a springboard to success.

Xylophones

I had to use at least one word actually beginning with 'x', so here we are! Children are often given little toy xylophones so you may have one lying around the house. Why not encourage your child to put their spellings to music and enjoy some multi-sensory spelling?

If they were learning some 'ck' words for example, the 'c' and the 'k' could be the same notes each time but your child could use different notes for the initial letter and the vowel. They could temporarily stick letter names on the notes to help them remember which note was which letter.

It could be fun for you to 'play' the spelling to your child and ask them if they can remember which word it is. Or you could ask them to sing the spelling once they have played it on the xylophone several times. When you think how easily we remember songs it is not surprising that putting spellings to music could help them to remember the spellings.

Y is for Yorkie the Lion and donkeys!

Extra materials needed:

- Colourful chocolate or cereal bar wrappers
- Computer and printer for printing out words in different fonts, sizes and colours
- Stopwatch

When I was teaching in York, the home of a famous sweet manufacturer and then a famous chocolate factory, some of my pupils were struggling to remember the spelling of 'work'. I decided that special measures were called for and I contacted the chocolate factory, explained the difficulty and asked if they could possibly send me some chocolate bar wrappers. They responded magnanimously and sent me a whole box full of bars!

The class was really motivated to work hard, and we saved the wrappers and in due course produced a display with a giant 'work' made out of wrappers. I hoped that the pupils would remember that letters in their home town of York were also found in the word 'work' and that the smell and taste of the chocolate would help to anchor the spelling in their memory.

Just in case that plan did not succeed, I had another cunning plan up my sleeve. I invited Yorkie the Lion, the mascot for York City Football Club, to come and work with the class one morning. To my surprise, the class was most suspicious about Yorkie and was convinced I had just asked one of the teachers to dress up as him. It was only when a photo of Yorkie with the class was printed on that week's match programme, they finally believed me and were suitably star-struck!

It can be worth using colourful wrappers in displays of certain spelling sounds. The novelty value adds to the fun and aids memory and the power of association to accelerate learning should never be underestimated.

A 'y' rule: The letter 'y' has three sounds:

1. It can be a consonant, as in 'yes' and 'yogurt'.

2. It can replace the long 'i' sound at the end of words, because no English word ends in 'i', as in 'my', 'sky' and 'dry'.

3. It can also replace the short 'i' sound at the end of words, as in 'very', 'happy' and 'pretty'.

Because 'y' can act as a vowel as well as a consonant, it is often called a half vowel. Sometimes, the short 'i' sound at the end of words is made by the combination of 'ey', especially after 'k' and 'n':

SPELLING MADE MAGIC – An A-Z of spelling tips and tricks

donkey	monkey	turkey	jockey
honey	money	kidney	journey
chutney	cockney	chimney	phoney
alley	valley	volley	barley
motley	medley	parsley	trolley
abbey	curtsey	osprey	jersey

Make a card game in the style of 'Donkey', collecting sets of four of the same colour. How to play:

There are enough cards for six players. Make sure that you have a set of four for each player taking part. Shuffle the cards well and deal out four cards to each player.

Each player looks at their hands and decides which set to collect. The first player then puts one of his unwanted cards face down in front of the player on his left. The second player picks up the card that has been placed in front of him. If it helps him build up a set he can keep it and discard a card to the player on his left, or discard the one he picked up.

Play continues in this way until one player lays down a set of four as quietly as he can. The other players must respond quickly, by putting all their cards down, whether or not they have completed a set of four. The last player to lay down their cards is the 'donkey'.
Reshuffle the cards and play again.

A 'y' acrostic: young

Young **O**rangutans **U**pset **N**ice **G**orillas

Your child may like to illustrate the picture evoked by this – or they may prefer to devise their own acrostic and illustrate that one instead.

A 'y' homophone: your /you're/yore

When I was young, I had to learn a poem by William Makepeace Thackeray which began;

"There lived a sage in days of yore
And he a handsome pigtail wore…."

'Yore', meaning 'long ago' is not a very common word and, indeed, is not even in my newest dictionary! Perhaps we can ignore that homophone and concentrate on the other two.

It is helpful to learn to spell 'you' and 'your' together, to appreciate the visual similarity despite their difference aurally. Your child will hopefully be quite confident with contractions after our work in Chapter C and will remember that 'you're' is a contraction of 'you are'.

A polysyllabic 'y' word: youth/ful/ness

We have come across three different ways of pronouncing the 'you' sound in different words above:

You and youth, your, young

For such words it is fun to make a speed challenge. Print out the words several times in different fonts and sizes and mount them on playing cards. Then time your child as you deal the cards quickly in front of them and they read the words. They could also time you doing the speed challenge too and involve other members of the family. I recommend speed challenges with other groups of words that look similar but have different pronunciations. Boys, in particular, respond to the timed competitive element and love to whittle seconds off their time!

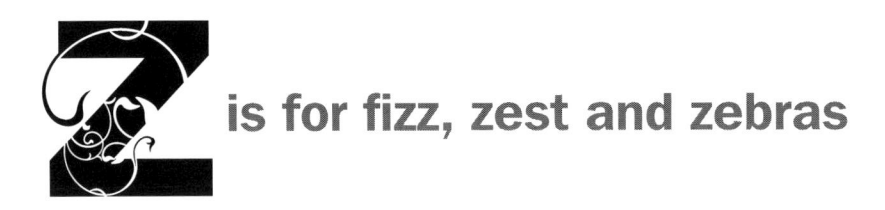

SPELLING MADE MAGIC – An A-Z of spelling tips and tricks

z is for fizz, zest and zebras

Extra materials needed:

Coloured card stars or gold or silver coloured card to make stars

So, here we are at the final chapter and I bet you are wondering what I can come up with for 'z'! Well, I have a zinging collection of 'z' words for you to put the pizazz into your last sprinkling of spelling magic!

A 'z' rule

Words with a short vowel ending in 'z' are 'flossy words' that double the final consonant. An exception is 'quiz'.

| buzz | fizz | fuzz | jazz | whizz |

If we add an ending like 'ed', 'ing' or 'y', we keep the double 'z'. Ask your child to zip these words together:

buzz + ing =   fizz + y = _

fuzz + y =   whizz + ing = _

buzz + er =   jazz + y =

There is quite a collection of two-syllable words ending in 'le' that contain the double 'z', although the first syllable does not make a word on its own. Ask your child to copy out these exercises and complete them:

ra
da → zzle
fra

fi
si → zzle
gri

nu
mu → zzle
pu

Interestingly, the words 'lizard', 'wizard' and 'hazard' do not double the 'z'.

When we add an 's' to 'zz' words to make them plural or because of the verb ending, we have to add 'es' because it is difficult to say 'buzzs' without making a second syllable, which needs a vowel. So we say 'buzzes'.

Add 'es' to these doing words:

buzz	fuzz
fizz	jazz
whizz	

When we add 'es' to make the word 'quiz' plural we have to double the 'z' to stop the magic 'e' changing the vowel – 'quizzes'.

SPELLING MADE MAGIC – An A-Z of spelling tips and tricks

Some 'z' homophones:

There are lots of words that contain a 'z', or sound as though they do, and many of them have sound-alikes:

Fleas and flees	The robber fl**ee**s through the t**ree**s.
	Fle**a**s jump **a**bout.
Shoes and shoos	You wear sho**e**s on your f**ee**t.
Laze and lays	
Baize and bays	
Daze, dais and days	
Raze, raise and rays	
A razor and eraser	
Praise and prays	

Your child may not be familiar with all these homophones and you may feel that they do not need to know them at the moment. Therefore, you may like to choose those homophones your child is likely to meet and discuss ways of differentiating them together. I have suggested some possibilities above, such as thinking of a phrase with matching sounds. There's a nice little tongue twister for you and your child to say as fast as you can –

"A flea feeds on blood. A flea feeds on blood. A fea fleeds on blood. A flea fleeds on blood....!"

Long 'z' words

There are a number of long words that sound as though they have a 'z' in them. In fact, the Americans sometimes spell them with a 'z' although in the English language we use a 's'. Such words end in 'ise':

advise   revise   realise   recognise   idealise

emphasise   idolise   synthesise

Other words that sound as though they contain a 'z' are words that actually end in 'asm' or 'ism':

spasm   chasm   enthusiasm   specialism

The other common ending that sounds as though it contains a 'z' is the suffix 'sion', found at the end of such words as:

vision   revision   television   occasion   conclusion

In Chapter C when we first looked at syllabification – or chopping long words into chunks – we mentioned the 'tion' suffix which crops up time and again in long words. The 'tion' suffix sounds like 'shun' but the 'sion' suffix sounds like 'zhun'.

An easy way to tell the suffixes apart is to put your fingers very gently against your Adam's apple and say a 'tion' word. Your fingers will feel nothing. However, if you say a 'sion' word your fingers will feel a slight buzzing sensation. Thus, if your child is unsure whether to spell the suffix of a word with 'tion' or 'sion' get them to do the Adam's apple test!

A dazzling zodiac of 'z' words

Your child may like to write the 'z' words we have used on coloured card stars that can be bought from most stationers or on gold or silver stars cut out from card. These stars can be stuck on your child's bedroom ceiling or around the walls, in the shapes of constellations or signs of the zodiac.

Zebras

In Chapter M we looked at the memory game 'My aunt went to market' and its variations, which proceed through the alphabet. As one goes through the alphabet, there are certain letters for which it is always difficult to find words – and one of those letters is 'z'. It is, therefore, worth having some words ready up your sleeve, like 'zebra', 'zip', 'zircon' and 'zucchini'. Even if you can only think of 'zebra', you can be quite creative with it and be given a zebra-striped hat for Christmas or eat zebra steaks or have a pet zebra. The memory game involves your child's imagination and creativity so they don't have to worry about being politically correct or truthful!

By sheer coincidence, as I was writing about zebras, one of my home tuition pupils came for her lesson, clutching a wonderful zebra pen! She was so keen to use it for her lesson and wrote with renewed enthusiasm. I would encourage you to collect novelty pens and use attractive glitter or gel pens to add colour and sparkle to spelling sessions. Do you remember the smelly pens from Chapter S? My pupils use furry pens, fluffy pens, feathery pens, quill pens, pencils with animal or bird heads, tiny pencils, big fat pencils and so on! Anything that injects enjoyment and novelty into writing is going to make spelling fun – and that's a big part of creating magical lessons.

Hopefully, after working through our spelling alphabet, some of the magic will have rubbed off on your child and they will have discovered a new zest for spelling. They should now be able to dazzle you with their spelling and to zap even the longest of words. They should be virtually fizzing over with confidence and buzzing with competence. To acknowledge your child's amazing achievement, there is an award certificate at the end of this book that you can sign and give to them. Then you can crack open the fizzy pop and have a party with pizzazz to celebrate what can be accomplished with just a little

Spelling Magic!

I'M A MAGIC SPELLER!

This certificate is awarded to:

- - - - - - - - - - - - - - - - - -

in recognition of

Achievement in making Spelling Magic!

Signature   Date

Spelling Made Magic glossary

Acrostics – Poems or sentences where the first letter of each word or line together spell a word, i.e. through – Ten Hairy Round Oranges Use Green Hairspray.

Digraph – A pair of letters representing a single speech sound, such as the 'sh' in shoe or the 'ea' in beat.

Homophone – Where two words sound the same but have different spellings, such as 'two' and 'too'.

Mnemonics – Mnemonics are simple phrases that make it easier to remember certain things. Eg. 'Richard of York Gave Battle In Vain' which can be used to remember the colours of the rainbow.

Phoneme – The smallest unit of speech which distinguishes one word (or word element) from another (e.g., the sound 'c' in 'cat', which differentiates that word from 'hat' and 'mat').

Prefix – Letters placed in front of a word to form a new word: e.g. 'bilingual', 'multilingual', 'address', 'redress', 'predate', 'postdate'.

Suffix – A letter or a group of letters added to the end of a word to change its meaning. For example, adding the suffix '-ger' to the adjective 'big' turns it into the comparative adjective 'bigger', and adding the suffix '-ly' to the adjective 'quick' turns it into the adverb 'quickly'.